VICTORY
OVER
ANXIETY

**Take Your
Anxious Thoughts
Captive**

Dr. Andrea Ganahl

Victory Over Anxiety:
Take Your Anxious Thoughts Captive
By Dr. Andrea Ganahl

Diagrams and back cover photo by Kayla Petrosky.

First Printing

Published by:
Andrea Ganahl
AndreaGanahl@AndreaGanahl.com

TESTIMONIALS

We all have experienced the debilitating effects of anxiety or have a loved one who is being affected. It can cripple a soul, a marriage, a family, and a career. Dr. Ganahl's ability to write from a personal and vulnerable level, yet with a high degree of clinical professionalism and biblical practicality, make this a must-read for anyone wanting information or help. There are great solutions in these pages. Highly recommended.

— John Townsend, Ph.D., *New York Times* bestselling author and psychologist. Founder, the Townsend Institute and the Townsend Leadership Group

Severe anxiety is a very painful physical and emotional experience to endure. Finding direct and practical advice is so needed for those who are suffering. In *Victory Over Anxiety*, Andrea puts together clear steps covering every necessary area for growth to overcome anxiety. *Victory Over Anxiety* is a great resource that many anxiety sufferers will deeply appreciate. Her personal and humorous approach is healing as well.

— Robyn L. Bettenhausen Geis, PsyD, psychologist and author of *The Relational Brain: A Path to Heal Broken Relationships*, and *Counseling and Mental Health in the Church*.

If you want to understand how to lessen your anxiety or have a loved one struggling with excessive worry, this book is the answer to your prayers. Dr. Ganahl will walk you through the steps to understand how your brain, body, and thought life can be challenged and changed, transforming you into a more tranquil person. You will learn how to renew your mind, change your thought patterns, challenge your inaccurate assumptions, and reframe your reactions to stress. She also addresses sleep patterns, nutritional elements, and the need for godly guidance. *Victory Over Anxiety* is a full spectrum approach to taming your anxiety. I thank God for her relatable, non-judgemental approach and her biblical wisdom.

— Nancy C. Anderson, marriage mentor and author of *Avoiding the Greener Grass Syndrome.*

I have known Dr. Ganahl for more than fifteen years. I'm not surprised that she presents the topic of anxiety in an extraordinary way. She responds to this epidemic that has taken significant portions of our youth and adult population by providing practical exercises to reduce anxiety. *Victory Over Anxiety* is an easy-to-follow, solution-based guide. The love with which Andrea writes to anxiety sufferers and the professional knowledge that is supported by the Word of God makes this book an exceptional tool.

— Fransisco Alonso, senior pastor of Misión El Camino, Costa Mesa, California

Incredibly insightful and immediately practical. The information and resources Dr. Ganahl provides will unburden you and create a clear path to reduced anxiety. If you have ever felt trapped by your anxious thoughts (as I have), I deeply encourage you to read *Victory Over Anxiety.*

— Doug Brown, co-founder of Uniquely Knitted, an infertility nonprofit

Dr. Andrea Ganahl takes the complex and often shame-filled topic of anxiety and shares practical and digestible tools that bring a sense of hope and normalcy. She doesn't talk down to you, and there is no shaming your experience or the legitimacy of your struggle. The way she communicates her vulnerability makes it feel like she is coming alongside the reader and that you are in it together. Andrea will teach you how to proactively adapt your daily routine to conquer anxiety-inducing circumstances that inevitably come along.

— Desiree Elrod, Prayer Counseling Ministry, Calvary Church Santa Ana

DEDICATION

To my father,
John Francis Drew,
who taught me to be generous
and to work hard.
Most importantly, he taught me
what true redemption looks like.
I miss you so much it hurts.

TABLE OF CONTENTS

SECTION I:
INTRODUCTION

"Who of you by worrying," [Jesus said,] "can
add a single hour to his life?"
— Matthew 6:27

It's two in the morning. My heart is racing, and I'm having a hard time catching my breath. I lay awake, thinking about my marriage. *What if we don't make it through our latest difficulty?* About my boys, *What if they don't come out of adolescence, okay? What if I have not been a good enough mother?* What if? What if? What if? I think about my dad's health. *What if he dies soon?* Or *What if he lives a long time with dementia?* That reminds me to think about my dear friend, who has cancer. *Lord, why do you allow such difficult circumstances?* That gets me thinking about other horrible conditions. *What about all the children dying of starvation around the world?* I realize I am hungry and think, *What if we have a natural disaster and I haven't prepared enough, and we all go hungry or die of thirst?* The anxious thoughts continue throughout the night.

Why can't I fall asleep? Why can't I stop torturing myself with these terrible thoughts? *Lord, help me. Please take away these thoughts of mine.*

"Dear child, you must take your thoughts captive to make them obedient to me."

Lord, I know that, but I can't seem to do it.

1

I have experienced anxiety much of my life. During that sleepless night, I realized I had to figure out how to take my anxious thoughts captive to live a more peace-filled life. To reduce my anxiety, I began to study, research, and pray about taking my anxious thoughts captive and renewing my mind. With a great deal of hard work through prayer, meditating on God's Word, and reaching out to godly women, I applied what I was discovering and learned how to reduce my anxiety significantly. I would like to say I am cured of anxiety, but let's be honest, there is no cure for anxiety. It is part of the human condition. We can, however, learn to manage anxiety and live a peace-filled, victorious life.

Anxiety is exhausting and in most cases, absolutely unnecessary. You probably have never thought, *Boy, I'm glad I worried about that for so long.* Or *My worrying about that changed the outcome.* How many times have you worried about something that *might* happen? and it never did. And for those few times that the bad thing happened, did the worrying ahead of time make any difference? Probably not. John Kavanaugh wrote in his book *The Word Engaged: Meditation on the Sunday Scriptures,* "If we could count the fears, both great and small, that once hounded us, and then thank God for each dreaded outcome that never materialized, we would reach no end of gratitude."[1]

We are not to be taken captive by our thoughts. Rather, we must take our thoughts captive, which is key to reducing anxiety. "We demolish arguments and every pretension that sets itself up against the knowledge of God, and we take captive every thought to make it obedient to Christ" (2 Corinthians 10:5).

The words "take captive every thought" describe an action we are to continuously do. It is not a one-time thing or a once-in-a-while action. We are to continually take our thoughts captive.

I pray that you will receive a great deal of encouragement from this book, and you will apply some of the ideas and exercises presented, all of which are proven to reduce anxiety. We cannot sit back and wait for change to occur. We must do the work to alter our way of thinking. God has blessed us with a fantastic mind, which allows us to think and choose. The number of possible choices we can make every day is endless.

Most importantly, we get to choose what thoughts we allow to linger in our minds. We have a choice. We can take our thoughts captive and make them obedient to Christ, or we can let our thoughts take hold of us, crippling us with anxiety. So if you are ready to learn how to take your anxious thoughts captive and allow God to heal your heart and mind, let's get started.

How to Best Use This Book

Victory over Anxiety is divided into four parts. The first part provides general information on anxiety. This information will teach you what anxiety is, the causes, and the various types of anxiety disorders. You will learn how the brain functions under anxiety and how we can rewire our brains to reduce anxiety.

Section Two is about the cognitive techniques we can use to lower anxiety. I will discuss the importance of captivating, evaluating, and renovating our minds. I will share where anxiety originates and how to change our belief system as well as our subconscious minds. Section Two is crucial to lasting change.

In Section Three, we will go over relaxation techniques. Relaxation exercises are an essential aspect of reducing anxiety. I say several times in Section Two to go to Section Three if you experience significant anxiety while practicing the various cognitive techniques. Relaxation is the beginning of reducing anxiety. I chose to put it after the cognitive techniques chapters, because I have found that many people want to get to the material's substance first. The "meat" is Section Two, but some people have difficulty completing the cognitive exercises without implementing relaxation. Therefore, if you have a hard time getting through the cognitive techniques, go to Section Three. After you get some relaxation exercises under your belt, you can return to Section Two. The cognitive techniques can bring up anxious feelings, while relaxation techniques lower the physical symptoms of anxiety significantly.

Part Four is about lifestyle modifications that can reduce anxiety. In these chapters, I discuss physical exercise, nutrition, and sleep as it relates to anxiety. I also have a chapter on implementing new habits. Don't skip these chapters. There is valuable information you need to know about lowering anxiety.

Lastly, I have a chapter on what God says about anxiety. There is encouragement in these pages, not condemnation. You will hear about godly men and women in the Scriptures who experienced anxiety.

CHAPTER 1
WHAT IS ANXIETY?
AND
WHAT ARE THE CAUSES?

Worry is like a rocking chair; it gives you
something to do, but it never gets you anywhere.
— Erma Bombeck

It's a beautiful spring day. I am standing outside, looking at the magnificent forest in Mount Hermon, California. Butterflies are flying around in my stomach. I feel nauseous. I am thinking, *Please don't throw up*. My legs feel weak. My hands are clammy. My breathing is shallow, and my heart is racing. I feel tension throughout my back and neck. I am sweating as if it is a ninety-degree day. I question my sanity. What is happening?

We experience anxiety for three reasons:

1. We are in real danger: a car is swerving into our lane.
2. We have a problem to solve: I'm anxious about a test coming up, so I need to study.
3. We have inaccurate thoughts: we believe something with no evidence to back it up.

Distorted thinking is the most common reason we experience anxiety. Therefore, our thought life will be our focus during our time together.

First we need to define what anxiety is—a challenging emotion, defined as *fear or nervousness about what might happen* (emphasis added).[2] Anxious thoughts usually start with *what if*. Many people with anxious thoughts also have vivid images that support their anxiety. We all experience anxiety and fear.

Fear is "a strong unpleasant feeling caused by being aware of danger or expecting something terrible to happen."[3] Fear is associated with a clear, present, and identifiable threat. The main difference between fear and anxiety is that fear includes an awareness of danger. When I talk about fear, worry, or anxiety, I'm referring to the *what-ifs* with which we battle. I am not talking about the fear we experience when we are in real danger or need to solve a problem. We need to be aware of *real* danger to survive. Most of what we struggle with regarding anxiety is inaccurately perceived danger or fears of the future, not life-threatening situations.

For example, the fear we experience when approached by a Rottweiler growling and baring his teeth is healthy and realistic. A thought that triggers this kind of fear might be, *This dog is aggressive and might bite me.* This thought is appropriate and can help us avoid a bite. However, if a Chihuahua is wagging its tail as it approaches us on a leash with its owner, and we feel intense fear, our thought process is off-base. You might be thinking, *Who cares if it's an unhealthy fear? I would rather be safe than sorry.* The problem is, when we experience an irrational fear, we have the same physical response as we would if we were in real danger. Our bodies go into the fight-flight-freeze mode either way.

The fight-flight-freeze response, also known as the stress response, is an automatic physical reaction that is activated when our mind perceives a dangerous situation.

A situation where I might need to fight would be if someone grabbed me and tried to push me into a car. I would fight with all my might to free myself. However, if I were in my home and an earthquake occurred, I would run for cover. The freeze response might happen if I saw a rattlesnake and didn't want to draw attention to myself. These situations can cause our bodies to react physically without any conscious effort. During a fight-flight-freeze response, some of the physical symptoms are: increased heart rate, sweaty palms, shallow and rapid breathing, muscle tension, and nausea. Do these symptoms sound similar to how you feel when you are anxious? If we are worried about something that *might* happen or something that is happening but isn't life-threatening, we will still have a fight-flight-freeze response. Our bodies cannot tell the difference between *perceived* danger and *real* danger. Repeated responses to hazards that aren't dangerous will take a toll on our bodies and our minds.

During my anxiety attack at Mount Hermon, I experienced a great deal of anxiety about what *might* happen. I was not in a life-threatening situation. I was attempting to work through my phobia of heights, so I was zip-lining.

To calm down, I took deep breaths. I attempted muscle relaxation, and I reminded myself of the Bible verses I had planned to say over and over in my mind. The memorizations that helped me with my anxious thoughts were: "So do not fear for I am with you; do not be dismayed for I am your God. I will strengthen you and help you; I will uphold you with my righteous right hand" (Isaiah 41:10). And, "'I know the plans I have for you,' declares the Lord, 'plans to prosper you and not to harm you, plans to give you hope and a future'" (Jeremiah 29:11).

I also informed the zip-line guides of my situation in case I threw up or passed out. Praise God. I did neither. The young men were compassionate as well as humorous, which helped me immensely.

The first zip-line was the easiest. The rides became higher and longer as we continued. I'm happy to say I did it. I may have screamed every time and hugged each tree I soared to, but I did it. I want to be honest with you. I did not enjoy myself, nor would I do it again, but I am delighted I reached my goal. My fear of heights is not gone, but I will experience less anxiety each time I expose my fear to a more relaxed body and mind. Working through my fear of heights will benefit me when I am on a ski lift or gondola or looking out a window from a high-rise.

Many levels of anxiety exist. Some are at a level that is considered a *disorder*. Don't let that scare you. Just because you experience anxiety doesn't mean you have a diagnosable anxiety disorder. Even if you do, there is no reason to be ashamed. As you will see, anxiety is a common issue in our mental well-being. We all feel anxious at times, and for some of us, a great deal of the time.

Forty million Americans suffer from an anxiety disorder. Women are twice as likely to be afflicted as men. Unfortunately, only one third of sufferers seek help. Also, there is strong evidence that people who suffer from anxiety are at a higher risk of developing several chronic health conditions.[4]

The Diagnostic and Statistical Manual of Mental Disorders V (DSM-5) is a manual mental health professionals use to determine if a person meets the criteria for a mental disorder. *The DSM-5* covers all categories of mental health illnesses for both adults and children. There are many anxiety disorders. Only a professional can evaluate an individual and determine the proper diagnosis.

Specific Phobia

Specific Phobia is the most common anxiety disorder affecting nineteen million Americans. Individuals suffering from a Specific Phobia diagnosis fear a particular object or situation, such as flying, heights, specific animals, enclosed spaces, or seeing blood. The phobic situation or object provokes immediate anxiety. Women are twice as likely to suffer from phobias as men. Symptoms typically begin in childhood.[5]

Social Anxiety Disorder

The second most common anxiety disorder, Social Anxiety Disorder (SAD), is a "marked fear of being exposed to possible scrutiny by others in social situations."[6] People who suffer from SAD experience enough anxiety to avoid most social situations or endure them with intense fear. SAD affects about fifteen million adults in the U.S. It is equally common among men and women. Social Anxiety Disorder often begins around the age of thirteen.[7]

General Anxiety Disorder

General Anxiety Disorder (GAD) is also common, affecting 6.8 million adults in the U.S.[8] GAD is what it sounds like, generalized anxiety that is excessive. Most worriers experience anxiety about an hour a day, while a person suffering from GAD suffers over five hours a day.[9] The worry is associated with at least three of the following symptoms: restlessness, easily fatigued, difficulty concentrating, irritability, muscle tension, and sleep disturbance. There must be significant clinical distress for at least six months to meet the criteria for this diagnosis.[10] Women are twice as likely to be affected as men. Major depression often coexists with GAD. Unfortunately, only 43.2 percent of people suffering from GAD seek treatment.[11]

Panic Disorder

Another form of anxiety is Panic Disorder, which is recurrent unexpected panic attacks. Intense fear peaks within minutes, with physical symptoms such as heart palpitations, sweating, shaking, nausea, and chest pain.[12] Also, people with Panic Disorder experience significant anxiety due to the fear that they will have another attack. Panic Disorder affects six million adults. Women are twice as likely to receive this diagnosis.[13]

Obsessive-Compulsive Disorder

Obsessive-Compulsive Disorder (OCD) is the presence of obsessions (recurrent and persistent thoughts) and/or compulsions (repetitive behaviors) that take up more than an hour per day or cause clinically significant distress or impairment.[14] OCD affects 1 percent of the U.S. population. A diagnosis of OCD is equally common among men and women. One-third of adults first experienced symptoms in childhood.[15] OCD is no longer on the list of anxiety disorders in the *DSM-5* because it is now its own disorder. Similarly, Posttraumatic Stress Disorder (PTSD) is no longer considered an anxiety disorder but rather a Trauma-and-Stressor-Related Disorder.

Posttraumatic Stress Disorder

PTSD is the response to a significant traumatic event associated with intrusive memories and dreams, avoidance of external reminders of the event, negative alterations in cognitions and moods regarding trauma, and a marked change in emotional arousal and reactivity. The symptoms must be present for at least one month after the trauma occurred.[16] The majority of people who experience severe trauma do not develop PTSD. Posttraumatic Stress Disorder affects 7.7 million adults in America.[17]

You may not have a diagnosable anxiety disorder even though you struggle with worry every day. It is the day-in and day-out worrying that takes its toll on our minds and bodies. We often focus on the worst-case scenario. Even if something good happens, we might say, "That's great, but what if . . . ?

I worked with a woman, and no matter how good things were, she would say, "But things could change at any moment." The *what-ifs* haunted her so much she couldn't enjoy anything positive. Worriers fear that if they take in the good, they might be disappointed. They need to prepare for the worst. That is not living.

So what do we do? We learn to take our anxious thoughts captive. Evaluate our thoughts to determine if they are healthy, and then renovate them by focusing on more accurate and healthy thinking. I'm not talking about a feel-good, power-of-positive-thinking bunch of foolishness. I'm talking about renewing our minds for a healthier thought life.

Causes of Anxiety

The causes of anxiety, like many other mental health issues, are not entirely understood. A traumatic or even mildly stressful event can trigger anxiety. A triggering event for one person may not be a triggering event for another. Here are some of the risk factors for anxiety:

- Trauma
- Adverse childhood experiences
- Stress due to illness and stress build-up
- Personality
- Other mental health issues (such as depression)
- Drugs and medication(use, abuse, or withdrawal)
- Medical conditions
- Genetics
- Learned Anxiety
- Thought Life

Let's take a look at some of these risk factors.

Trauma

Trauma is not only a common cause of anxiety, but it is also a multifaceted factor. Trauma is an emotional response to a challenging event like war, an accident, rape, or natural disaster. An individual may experience trauma as a response to any event they find physically or emotionally threatening or harmful.[18] An event doesn't have to be catastrophic to be traumatic. Some of the feelings a person who has gone through a traumatic event may experience are: overwhelmed, helpless, shocked, afraid, or sad. If symptoms persist, PTSD may develop.

It is essential to understand that most people who experience a traumatic event, even a catastrophic event, do not develop PTSD. Studies have looked at why some people who experience the same event, like a natural disaster or terrorist attack such as 9/11, did not develop PTSD while others did. The studies found that those who participated in the following behaviors did not endure long-term suffering.

- Continued contact with support from important people in their lives
- Disclosed trauma to loved ones
- Identified as a survivor instead of a victim
- Used positive emotions and laughter
- Found post-meaning in trauma
- Helped others in their healing process
- Believed they could manage their feelings and cope[19]

Many other factors influence whether a person will develop PTSD. Trauma is a very complex issue.

Adverse Childhood Experiences

Adverse Childhood Experiences (ACE) are potentially traumatic events that occur in childhood. They can result in trauma and chronic stress responses. The higher a person's ACE score, the more vulnerable they are to mental and physical health problems in adulthood. The ten widely recognized ACEs are: physical abuse, sexual abuse, verbal abuse, emotional neglect, physical neglect, caregivers with alcohol or drug problems, caregivers with mental health problems, domestic violence, caregivers who have spent time in prison, and parents who have separated or divorced. Of course, many other difficult childhood experiences can harm a child. Sixty-one percent of adults surveyed have experienced at least one type of ACE, and nearly one in six reported having four or more Adverse Childhood Experiences.

Stress Due to Illness and Stress Build-up

Stress due to illness, as well as stress build-up, can create anxiety. Any time we are overwhelmed with stress, we are vulnerable to mental health issues. Think of your emotional capacity as a stream. The water—in this case, everyday stress—flows calmly down the stream. However, if a massive storm floods the stream, the stream will overflow its typical path and cause havoc to the surrounding area. Too much water at once will overwhelm the stream. In the same way, too much stress will overwhelm our capacity to respond healthily.

Personality

Certain personality traits are more susceptible to anxiety. People who have a more perfectionistic style are at a higher risk of experiencing anxiety. When we have unrealistic expectations, we tend to worry about things that are not just right. Also, perfectionists have a significant amount of anxiety about how others perceive them. Some say fear creates a perfectionistic style, while others believe perfectionism develops anxiety. Either way, they seem to go hand in hand.

Introverts tend to have an increased risk for anxiety. Introverts have a higher level of sensitivity to external stimulation, which produces higher fear levels.

Other Mental Health Issues

Other mental health issues are common with anxiety. Having more than one mental health issue is called *comorbidity*. The comorbidity of anxiety and depression is one of the most common mental health diagnoses. It is estimated that 60 percent of people suffering from anxiety also struggle with depression and vice versa.[20]

Approximately 20 percent of individuals with an anxiety disorder also struggle with substance abuse and vice versa. Thirty percent of people suffering from social anxiety disorder also abuse alcohol. It seems, for some, alcohol eases anxiety in social situations. However, alcohol abuse creates additional problems.

Drugs and Medication

Drugs and medications that can cause anxiety are: alcohol and illegal drugs such as cocaine and LSD; nonprescription medications such as decongestants; caffeine; prescription medications such as stimulants, steroids, and medicines that treat asthma, Parkinson's disease, and thyroid problems.[21]

People have asked me many times if marijuana can create anxiety. Marijuana consists of two main ingredients: THC, the psychotropic compound responsible for the high one gets using marijuana, and CBD, the non-psychotropic compound used for numerous therapeutic reasons. The consensus seems to be that CBD can lower anxiety, and possibly low doses of CBD with THC may help. However, higher dosages of THC can increase anxiety and even trigger paranoia in some individuals.

Medical Conditions

Some medical conditions can cause anxiety. The illnesses are: rare types of tumors, hyperthyroidism, some infectious diseases such as Lyme's disease, untreated strep, poor nutrition, head trauma, heart disease, diabetes, chronic pain, and COPD. Other areas are hormone inbalance of estrogen, progesterone, testosterone, stress hormones, thyroid hormones, or oxytocins. Vitamin B-12 deficiency can also produce anxiety, which we will discuss in more detail in Chapter 14, "Nutrition and Mental Health." If you think your anxiety may be due to a medical issue or prescription medications, discuss your concerns with your doctor.

Genetics

Genetics can potentially influence some mental health issues, including anxiety. Researchers have been studying the connection between anxiety and genetics for decades. However, it isn't easy to separate how much is due to genetics versus the environment.

Learned Anxiety

Anxiety can be learned. Children of anxious parents often become anxious themselves. Unfortunately, I have an example of this in my own life. When my first child was born, I was a nervous wreck. My husband and I had gone through five years of infertility. When my son John was born, unknown to me, I was responding to some unprocessed, emotional baggage connected to my infertility journey. It is hard for me to describe how excited I was to finely have a child. I wanted to protect my son from any danger, including but not limited to the concrete, the step stool, the street, choking, the pool, an unkind child, and of course, the possible pedophile lurking around the corner. As a toddler, John was afraid of many things. I didn't understand how he could be anxious when I was protecting him from everything.

One day, we were at my parent's home, in and around their pool. Ever so carefully, my son walked around the pool, because he was so afraid of falling in, even though he was a good swimmer. I went inside while my mom and sister kept an eye on the kids. When I returned, my mother told me how different John acted when I wasn't present. "He was much more carefree," she said.

What was that supposed to mean? I went back inside and watched from a window. She was right. My son was running around the pool, playing and having a great time. I was heartbroken for John. I couldn't believe I had created so much anxiety in him. John had the natural tendency to be an anxious person, but I became aware that my fears made his anxiety much worse.

By the time my second son was a toddler, I was more relaxed. I am thankful for that, because my second son is active and a thrill-seeker. When he was three years old, he had to get stitches three months in a row. After his third set of stitches, he was on a four-foot-high stone wall. I asked him if he thought being on the wall was a good idea. His response was, "It's okay, mommy. If I fall, I will just get more stitches." I have lost count of how many stitches and broken bones my boys have endured. These experiences actually helped me be more at ease around my boys, which allowed them to be more free.

Thought Life

Another highly-regarded cause of anxiety is related to our thought life. The way we think can create anxiety. Our thought life, in relation to anxiety, will be the focus of this book.

How much anxiety do you have? If you are interested in determining how much anxiety you are currently experiencing, go to my website at www.AndreaGanahl.com, click on Blogs and go to The Burns Anxiety Inventory. You can print it out and take the test. You will find the breakdown of scores there as well. As you implement the exercises in the chapters that follow, I encourage you to retake the inventory and see if your score decreases. Having victory over anxiety takes time. Give yourself grace and compassion.

Application:

When you notice you have an anxious thought, take three deep breaths, breathing in through your nose and out through your mouth. Focus on the breath itself. Feel the air coming in through your nostrils. Hold your breath for three seconds and then push the air out, noticing the breath leave your mouth. In Chapter 9, I will discuss how to use deep breathing to relax and reduce anxiety.

Questions:

1. Have you ever experienced something similar to what I experienced when I went zip-lining? If so, what symptoms did you have? Take a few minutes to write your experience and then share it with a friend or family member when you get a chance.

_____

_____

_____

2. Do any of the causes of anxiety we discussed apply to you? If so, which one(s)?

_____

_____

_____

CHAPTER 2
ESSENTIAL BRAIN FUNCTIONS REGARDING ANXIETY

The human brain has 100 billion neurons, each neuron connected to 10 thousand other neurons, sitting on your shoulders is the most complicated object in the known universe. — Michio Kaku

As I walked through the mall with my three-year-old and nine-month-old boys, my older son, John, spotted Santa Claus. I was so desperate to get out of the house I had forgotten John was afraid of Santa. A few days before our trip to the mall, John said, "I don't want that man with the white beard and red outfit coming down our chimney. He can leave my presents on the porch." When John saw Santa, he screamed, kicked me in the shin, and threw himself on the floor.

I remembered the parenting class I had taught. My first thought was, *Jesus, please don't let anyone from that class be here to observe this scene.* My next thought was, *Why didn't I take the boys to the zoo?* Then I thought, *This meltdown has happened before, although never with the kicking of my shin. John's fear has taken over his ability to think clearly.* A few curse words may have been sprinkled in all my thoughts.

I went into action, hoping to save myself from any further embarrassment. I asked John, "How high can you count?"

He stopped flailing on the floor and said, "What?"

I repeated myself, and then he started counting.

I knew I didn't have much time before he remembered why he was on the floor, so I picked him up, encouraged him to keep counting, and left the mall. This event occurred before I understood the benefits of exposure.

John's reaction to seeing Santa was based on what was happening in his brain.

The three areas of the brain I want us to understand for anxiety reduction are the frontal lobe, specifically the prefrontal cortex (PFC), the amygdala, and the anterior cingulate.

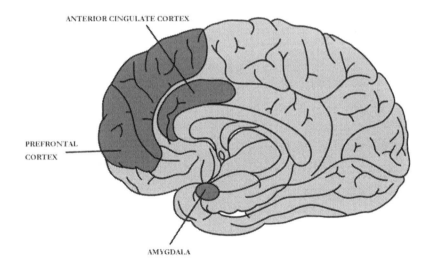

Prefrontal Cortex

Some of the PFC functions are concentration, planning, judgment, emotional expression, and decision-making. The prefrontal cortex is not only a part of the brain that is responsible for higher forms of thinking and decision making, but it also allows us to learn from experience. When we are undergoing a significant amount of emotion, our PFC becomes disengaged, making it difficult to think clearly and rationally. John's PFC became disengaged when he saw Santa. The moment we reengage our PFC, also known as the *thinking brain*, we are more able to manage our emotions. Asking John to count helped him reengage his thinking brain. The PFC also plays a vital role in encoding and retrieving memories. One last important fact, especially regarding adolescence and the PFC: the prefrontal cortex is not fully developed until our mid-twenties. This might help explain the decision making and *crazy-making* of the teenage years.

Amygdala

The amygdala is the size of an almond, located deep in our brains (see above diagram). We have one in each hemisphere. The primary function of the amygdala is associated with fear. The amygdala is involved in all anxiety, both amygdala-based anxiety and cortex-based anxiety. It is also crucial in forming and storing memories of emotional events. The amygdala is part of the limbic system, which performs the brain's emotional work. Think of the amygdala as our *protector*. It is continually receiving information from our five senses to determine if there is any danger. The amygdala gets this information earlier than the cortex, kicking us into the flight-fight-freeze response. This whole process takes a tenth of a second. The amygdala is so much faster than the cortex at spotting danger, because it directly connects to our five senses. You might be walking down the street and in your peripheral vision notice a car coming at you. Your amygdala will trigger the fight-flight-freeze response which will allow you to jump out of the way immediately. Your body automatically responds before your thinking brain does. Because of this process, many of us are alive today. Once the amygdala triggers the physiological reaction to the actual or perceived danger, it notifies the cortex.

This physiological response occurs when our amygdala is stimulated by perceived danger or any thoughts that create concern. As I mentioned in Chapter 1, the physiological reactions include increased heart rate and blood pressure, rapid shallow breathing, sweating, stomach distress, and muscle tension. Also, certain hormones increase as a result of the amygdala being stimulated. These are: adrenalin, cortisol (stress hormone), insulin, and our thyroid hormones.

On the positive side, when we have good thoughts, our body will secrete hormones such as serotonin and other chemicals that facilitate peace, happiness, love, and affection.

A fascinating fact about the amygdala: it can grow as a result of stress. The larger the amygdala, the more reactive it becomes. The good news is that we can reverse the size by implementing the techniques that calm the amygdala, such as; sufficient sleep with adequate REM sleep (see Chapter 15), regular physical exercise (see Chapter 13), and relaxation techniques (see Chapters 11 and 12).

The more reactive the amygdaly is, the more anxiety we will experience. The amygdala can override the prefrontal cortex and therefore, rational thinking. In other words, a highly charged amygdala can neutralize the PFC. Our emotions can disconnect our ability to think clearly. Consequently, the PFC and the amygdala counteract each other. To reduce anxiety, we need to apply techniques that stimulate the PFC.

Think back to a time when someone you cared about *lost control* of their emotions. Maybe he ranted and raved about something and said things he would usually not say. Or perhaps he kicked you in the shin. When this happens, he is disengaged from his rational mind. To help get him back *in control*, trigger his PFC. We can do this by asking him a math question or ask him to count, as I did with John. You can ask him to recall what he had for breakfast yesterday—any *who, what, where,* or *when* question works for most people. However, do not ask a *why* question, because that can trigger more emotion. A few mindful deep breaths can also activate the PFC. By the way, this is not a miracle cure for tantrums or an anxiety meltdown. In general, it puts a person's thinking cap on just long enough for them to calm down.

Highly anxious people have asked me if they can have their amygdala surgically removed to get rid of their anxiety. The answer is no. Although the amygdala is always involved when we experience fear, it is also responsible for feelings of love, joy, and awe. Without the amygdala, we would not bond with people. Next time you are frustrated with your amygdala, remember that it provides us with our most valuable emotions.

Anterior Cingulate

The anterior cingulate is partly responsible for how we filter reality. It allows us to process whether we are safe or a threat exists, based solely on sensory data such as what we see, hear, touch, smell, or even taste. Unlike the amygdala, which can grow due to stress, the anterior cingulate can shrink due to high anxiety and depression levels. We want our amygdala to stay small, about the size of an almond, but the opposite is true for our anterior cingulate. We want to keep this part of our brain from reducing in size. If it does decrease in volume, the electrical activity can diminish. When this happens, its functioning lessens. We no longer base our decisions on sensory information but on previous experiences that are generally inaccurate in determining a real threat. Therefore, we believe we are in danger when in reality we are not. Many of the exercises discussed in the coming chapters will help decrease the amygdala's size and increase the volume of the anterior cingulate.

A man went into a movie theater and started shooting, killing twelve people and injuring seventy. The shocking event was all over the news. Chances are pretty high that you have never been shot in a movie theater. However, if you remember hearing about this horrific incident, you probably thought about the tragedy the next time you went to the movies. This fear was learned by exposure to the trauma via the media. If we are in a movie theater, we should find nothing to fear using our five senses. However, as soon as we recall the news feed, we might go into the fight-flight-freeze mode. We are no longer filtering our reality correctly and are in this stress response for no logical reason.

Here is a summary of the three areas of the brain connected to anxiety:

Prefrontal Cortex

- Responsible for concentration, planning, judgment, emotional expression, and decision making
- Also known as the thinking brain
- Is not fully developed until our mid-twenties

Amygdala

- Associated with fear, and forming and storing memories of emotional events
- Is involved in all anxiety
- When stimulated, physiological responses are: increase in heart rate and blood pressure, rapid and shallow breathing, sweat, and muscle tension
- It can grow as a result of stress
- Involved in the emotional work of the brain and can override PFC

Anterior Cingulate

- Responsible for how we filter reality
- Decides if there is a threat based on sensory input
- Shrinks due to high levels of anxiety and depression

In addition to the three parts of the brain we have discussed regarding anxiety, some knowledge about the autonomic nervous system (ANS) might help. The ANS has a significant impact on the levels of anxiety we experience. The ANS regulates the body's subconscious actions. The ANS has two main parts: the sympathetic nervous system (SNS) and the parasympathetic nervous system (PNS).

The SNS regulates our fight-flight-freeze or stress response and is triggered when we perceive a threat. The threat might be genuine, in which we need to respond immediately, or it could be a learned threat that does not have any real merit. My son's SNS was activated when he saw the scary man in the red suit, even though Santa was not a real danger. When we worry about non-essentials, we decrease our ability to use this healthy fear response. When we use our imaginations to contemplate everything we *think* we should be afraid of, we ignore our surroundings.

In his book *The Gift of Fear*, Gavin DeBecker puts it this way: "Anytime your dreaded outcome cannot be reasonably linked to pain or death, and it isn't a signal in the presence of danger, then it really shouldn't be confused with fear. It may well be something worth trying to understand and manage, but worry will not bring solutions. It will more likely distract you from finding solutions."[22]

The PNS is responsible for decision making, concentration, sleep, digestion, and other activities that occur during rest. It is also responsible for the relaxation response. Only one of these two systems can be active at a time. Either our SNS is operating, which means we are stressed and in a fight-flight-freeze response, or our PNS is activated, and we are relaxed, our bodies functioning as they should. Except for those who work in a life-threatening job or are in a hazardous environment, our bodies rarely need to be in the fight-flight-freeze mode. If we continuously perceive threats that are not real, which is what most anxiety is, we will exhaust our bodies and compromise our health.

Therefore, learning to keep our PNS dominant is essential. We can do this by staying relaxed and out of the fight-flight-freeze response. The more relaxed our bodies are, the less anxiety we will experience, and the more we can use our thinking mind. The more we use our rational mind, the more we reduce our anxiety. The snowball effect can be very positive. The chapters that follow will give exercises that promote our bodies to be PNS dominant.

In summary:

Automatic Nervous System (ANS)

- It has a massive impact on anxiety.
- Regulates subconscious action.
- Its two main parts are the SNS and PNS.

Sympathetic Nervous System (SNS)

- Regulates fight-flight-freeze response.
- Only triggered when we perceive a threat.

Parasympathetic Nervous System (PNS)

- Responsible for decision making, concentration, sleep, digestion, and other activities that occur during rest.
- SNS or PNS cannot be activated at the same time.
- We want our bodies in PNS unless there is real danger.

We are fearfully and wonderfully made (Psalm 139:14 paraphrase).

Two Pathways to Anxiety

Now that you understand how the brain works, I want to explain the two pathways to anxiety. The cortex-based pathway is what most people think of when experiencing anxiety. The cortex is the thinking and processing part of the brain.

Cortex-Based Anxiety

- Is what most therapists, including myself, focus on when working with individuals suffering from anxiety
- Is the pathway of sensations, thoughts, logic, imagination, intuition, conscious memory, and planning
- Occurs through our five senses, external events, or our thoughts and images' internal events
- Is primarily a thought process

Your thinking creates anxiety—the what-if thoughts that spin around in your head. Because cortex-based anxiety is usually happening in the conscious mind, it is often much easier to treat. All the techniques in this book help reduce cortex-based anxiety.

Amygdala-Based Anxiety

The second pathway to anxiety is directly through the amygdala, bypassing the cortex. The amygdala is involved in all anxiety. However, with the cortex pathway, the anxiety starts in the cortex, which then triggers the amygdala. The amygdala-based pathway begins in the amygdala, which immediately triggers the physical responses, and then the cortex is ignited. As I mentioned earlier, the amygdala is responsible for the fight-flight-freeze reaction (rapid heart rate, rapid shallow breathing, muscle tension, and nausea).

Thoughts and images trigger cortex-based anxiety, whereas amygdala-based anxiety seems to show up out of nowhere. There is no conscious connection to a trigger. Instead, you are suddenly experiencing intense physical symptoms. It could begin in your stomach, or your breathing, or your muscles, or all over. You know you are anxious, but it's not due to your thoughts or images. You just *feel* intense fear. Therefore, many cognitive techniques are not effective in lowering this kind of anxiety. However, it is still helpful to learn cognitive-behavioral exercises, because even though amygdala-based anxiety starts without much cortex involvement, the cortex does end up being involved. For example, suddenly, you are experiencing the physical aspects of anxiety and are not sure what caused such a response. Then you begin to have anxious thoughts about what might happen next.

If your amygdala responds to something other than real danger, it is because of a learned response. Something happened previously in the environment that the amygdala associated with danger. What the amygdala connects the hazard to is called a *trigger*. Something that was once neutral becomes anxiety-provoking.

For example, Sharon is walking down the street, and a man walks by who is wearing Polo cologne. She immediately panics. Her legs feel weak, her stomach is in knots, her heart is racing, and she begins to hyperventilate. Later that evening, as she processes her experience, she recalls that the man who sexually assaulted her five years prior was wearing that same cologne. Polo cologne was a neutral stimulus until the amygdala associated it with the sexual assault.

Identifying the cause becomes much more challenging when someone experiences amygdala-based anxiety without the ability to pinpoint the trigger. Amygdala-based anxiety can happen if the trauma occurred before explicit memory developed (see Chapter 7) or some disassociation happened during the trauma. Also, during a stressful event, we are not usually attuned to everything going on around us. We may not remember the color of the car that hit the cyclist, but our amygdala remembers. Amygdala-based anxiety can occur for other reasons besides trauma. Any stressful event can have triggers. The stressful event doesn't even have to be something we experience. It can be something we saw on the news or heard about elsewhere.

Because amygdala-based anxiety responds to a learned fear, exposure is an important technique to lower this type of anxiety. In addition to exposure, relaxation techniques are crucial for healing amygdala-based anxiety. All the relaxation techniques, physical exercise, healthy sleep, and nutritional tips I discuss in future chapters will lower the amygdala's reactivity.

Identify Your Anxiety Type

We can tell if our anxiety is amygdala-based or cortex-based by determining what was happening right before we experienced the anxiety. Cortex-based anxiety occurs when we are focusing on specific thoughts or images. Whereas with amygdala-based, there is a sudden, unexpected physical anxiety reaction. It happens when a specific object, location, or situation elicits anxiety due to the amygdala's association with a previous experience. Often, we are unaware of what caused this sudden onset of anxiety symptoms.

Many times, panic attacks are amygdala-based. When in a panic attack, it is challenging to talk yourself out of anxiety due to the hijacked amygdala. Here are a few activities that may help: Try to activate your cortex. Then attempt to implement deep breathing. Take several slow, deep breaths. During a panic attack, do not hold your breath during the deep-breathing exercise. Also, try to relax your muscles. A relaxed body is a calm body. I know these two activities go against what your body wants to do. However, as you will see in later chapters, muscle relaxation and slow, deep breathing tell your amygdala you are okay, even if you don't *feel* okay. Third, go for a brisk ten-minute walk. I know that sounds crazy, but burning off the adrenaline the stress response dumped into your body can create calm. Additionally, attempt to distract yourself with something that triggers your thinking brain. Focusing on the symptoms will fuel the anxiety in an attack. And remember, a panic attack will not physically hurt you. It will pass, and you will survive.

Application:

Tighten all the muscles in your body. Hold the tension for three seconds. Then relax. Notice how your body reacts when it is tense, and then notice how it responds to being relaxed. Do this three times and see how you feel.

Questions:

1. What part of the brain did you find most intriguing? Why?

_____

_____

_____

2. Do you find yourself perceiving danger when there is none? If so, what events tend to trigger this perception?

_____

_____

_____

CHAPTER 3
THERE IS HOPE: THE WIRING AND REWIRING OF OUR BRAINS

Any man could if he were so inclined, be the
sculptor of his own brain.
—*Santiago Ramon y Cajal*

A few years ago, I attended the funeral reception of a friend's father. Sitting with several friends, I suggested we each tell a childhood story. Maybe that wasn't the best conversation starter at a funeral.

Marty was the first to respond. He told several heartbreaking stories about the absence of his parents. He was an emotionally healthy guy who was able to talk about how those experiences allowed him to be a more involved father himself.

Julie said she didn't have any problematic childhood experiences. We encouraged her to tell any story. She ended up telling three sad stories and then said, "Wow! I guess I did have some challenges in my childhood."

The motivation behind my suggestion was not to have us experience sadness about our childhood wounds but rather to know one another better. I never said anything about telling painful stories. However, every narrative was sad. That day, Julie learned that there is freedom in truth. She didn't feel sorrowful about her stories but believed she understood her life experiences better. God tells us in his Word, "Know the truth, and the truth will set you free" (John 8:32). Understanding why we think the way we do and knowing the truth about our hearts and minds can free us from anxiety.

What happened around the table that day is called the *negativity bias*. Negativity bias refers to the idea that we focus more on our negative experiences than we do neutral or positive ones. Something positive will generally have less impact on a person than something equally emotional but negative. Our brains are wired with Velcro for *bad* experiences and Teflon for *good* experiences. In simple terms, bad things stick, and good things, not as much. God created us this way to make it easier to survive the dangers of our environment. Remembering the sound of an angry bear is more important than the sound of a purring cat. When we are changing lanes, the sound of a car horn is more important than an ice cream truck's ringing bell. Negativity bias is why, when asked about childhood memories, we recall the negative ones more easily.

Our negative experiences are more strongly connected in our brains than our positive experiences due to this bias. How our experiences become deeply-wired in our brains is determined by how much we attend to them. The more we think, feel, and do something, the deeper and stronger the pathway becomes.

You probably have dinners you make without ever looking at the recipe. You can do this because you have made them so many times, they are etched in your memory. You can sing your favorite songs from twenty years ago, because you listened to them so often that they are deeply rooted in your brain. When we repeatedly have anxious thoughts, the feelings of anxiety become ingrained in our minds as well. Therefore, we are more vulnerable to feelings of anxiety.

My sister, Tina, and I hike several times a week. Most of the year, the trails are easy to follow, because they are well-traveled. However, in the winter and spring, the Southern California vegetation is more overgrown from the little bit of rain we get, and fewer people are hiking the trails. Therefore, maneuvering through the brush is more challenging. The more the trails are traveled, the easier it is to find our way, which happens with our brains' neuropathways. The more we use specific pathways, the more efficiently our minds follow that path.

Our brains contain billions of pathways. Some are deep and heavily traveled. Others are thin and weak, because they are rarely stimulated. The more we use a path, the more robust, more in-depth, and more accessible it is. Regarding anxiety pathways, the more we experience anxious thoughts, the more those pathways will be used, and the more likely they will be triggered again and again. Hence Dr. Hebb's rule: "Neurons that fire together wire together."[23] The good news is, if we develop skills to relax and be calm and learn to take our anxious thoughts captive, we can prune the anxiety pathways due to a lack of use. Isn't that exciting? We can prune the destructive paths.

This idea of pruning reminds me of Jesus being our true vine. Jesus says, "I am the true vine, and my Father is the gardener. He cuts off every branch in me that bears no fruit, while every branch that does bear fruit he prunes so that it will be even more fruitful" (John 15:1–2). He later says he is the vine and we are the branches (verse 5, author paraphrase). God wants to prune the areas in our lives that do not bear fruit. He wants to prune our anxiety.

We can prune our destructive pathways due to a process called *neuroplasticity*, which is the ability of our brains to change and adapt in response to experiences. We can change our neuropathways and introduce new experiences into our lives. We can also alter our brain's pathways by taking our destructive thoughts captive. Neuroplasticity is affected by how often we use specific pathways, how we attend to our life experiences, and how we care for ourselves through diet, exercise, and sleep.

It is important to note that neuroplasticity works both ways. It can work for us, because it allows us to prune adverse pathways and create new, healthier ones. However, neuroplasticity can work against us too. An extreme example would be what we see with PTSD. A person with PTSD relives the trauma repeatedly in his thought life, which causes the memory to become more deeply wired in the brain with each flashback.

Breaking our patterns of anxiety is essential. We must learn to captivate, evaluate, and renovate our thoughts to stop the cycle of destructive thinking.

Application:

Write down one or two anxious thoughts you regularly have. Start to be aware of how often you experience these thoughts. When we discuss cognitive-behavioral techniques, in later chapters, you can use these frequent thoughts in the exercises.

_____

_____

_____

Questions:

1. Have you noticed the negativity bias in yourself or others? If so, what did it look like.

_____

_____

_____

2. Are you ready to prune some of your anxiety pathways? If so, what pathways do you want to work on pruning?

_____

_____

_____

SECTION II:
HOW TO TAKE YOUR
ANXIOUS THOUGHTS CAPTIVE

The greatest weapon against stress is our ability
to choose one thought over another.
— William James

Let's look at cognitive and behavioral practices, which we can implement to reduce our anxiety. These principles have improved my life spiritually, emotionally, and physically. I use these techniques daily. We are to take *every* thought captive, not just our *anxious* thoughts. Therefore, we can apply these exercises many times a day. While I present many ideas, I encourage you to try as many as possible to discover which ones work best for you.

I will be asking you to practice the exercises in this section. If you feel a significant amount of anxiety at any time, please stop, go to Chapter 12, and practice the deep breathing and muscle relaxation techniques presented. These exercises should help reduce your anxiety enough to participate in the cognitive methods. I want to stress the importance of writing your responses to these exercises. Writing accomplishes many things:

1. Consolidates your thoughts and helps form memories.
2. Adds clarity to your thoughts.

3. Makes it easier to see cognitive distortions.
4. Ignites the pre-frontal cortex.
5. Allows you to revisit your work as well measure your progress.
6. Adds to the rehearsal of your healthy thoughts, which is needed to bring those thoughts into the subconscious mind.

In the first part of this section, I will discuss three essential steps to change the way we think in order to reduce anxiety. They are also necessary to decrease unhealthy and destructive thoughts that impact our overall mental health. We first need to *captivate* our thoughts, then *evaluate* them, and finally, we need to *renovate* our thoughts.

In the second part of Section II, I will discuss how our belief system affects our anxiety and how making changes at the subconscious level can tackle anxiety at its root. In the last part of this section, I will share additional cognitive-behavioral techniques you can implement daily to keep fear at bay.

Before we get started on Section II, I want to encourage you with "The Serenity Prayer," which is much more than a prayer for addicts. We can all benefit from applying this prayer to our daily lives.

> *God grant me the serenity to accept the things I*
> *cannot change, the courage to change the things I*
> *can, and the wisdom to know the difference.*
> — *Reinhold Niebuhr*

"The Serenity Prayer" encourages us to do three things: accept, be courageous, and develop wisdom. Who doesn't want to be more accepting, courageous, and wise? I know I do. If we accept the things we cannot change, we are transformed on the inside. Acceptance creates peace. Fighting against things that are out of our control creates anxiety.

Being courageous to change the things that need to be changed will lower fear and build self-confidence. Remember, courage does not *replace* fear. Courage *overcomes* fear. Every time we face our fears, we are developing more courage, which allows us to become who we want to be.

Developing the wisdom to know the difference between what we cannot change and what we can is crucial for a healthy thought life. Sometimes it's hard to know. But as we learn to evaluate our thoughts, circumstances, and resources, we can better understand what we need to accept and what we need to change. The most important part of this prayer is the first five words: "God grant me the serenity." We get to seek him for peace, for he himself is our peace (Ephesians 2:14).

CHAPTER 4
THREE STEPS TO CHANGE
HOW WE THINK

We demolish arguments and every pretension
that sets itself up against the knowledge of God,
and we take captive every thought to make it
obedient to Christ. — 2 Corinthians 10:5

I am excited to go home to sunny Southern California after visiting my grandmother in Iowa. So far, the flight is uneventful. I am enjoying my book when suddenly the plane drops, what feels like hundreds of feet (it was probably only ten). I panic. I think, *We are going down!* I hear the pilot's soothing voice over the intercom: "Ladies and gentleman, everything is fine. Just a little turbulence." I think, *A little turbulence? More like the engine exploded.* I can be a bit dramatic. Although everything seems to have calmed down, I am a wreck. My anxious thoughts are out of control. I am confident the plane will go down at any moment. Although we are not over the ocean, somehow I determine that we will crash into the sea. I decide I will not die when we hit the water. Instead, I will be savagely eaten by sharks.

My stomach is in knots, and I think I might need to use the bathroom. I finally say to myself, *Andrea Rose Ganahl* (I use my full name when I need to get my attention), *get your thoughts under control.* I remind myself that I am a psychologist specializing in anxiety. *For crying out loud, take your thoughts captive!*

I know I need to get my prefrontal cortex involved and implement relaxation techniques to captivate, evaluate, and renovate my thinking to reduce my anxiety. I begin my deep breathing as well as some muscle relaxation. I recall the statistic I looked up for an occasion such as this: my chances of dying in a single commercial flight are one in 29.4 million. I remember Deuteronomy 31:6. "Be strong and courageous. Do not be afraid or terrified because of them, for the Lord your God goes with you; he will never leave you nor forsake you."

I begin to calm down. I continue my deep breathing, and I pull out a crossword puzzle to keep my frontal lobe engaged.

The techniques I present come from Cognitive Behavior Therapy (CBT), a theory that states: our cognitions or thoughts and beliefs determine our emotions and behaviors. Therefore, how and what we think affects how we feel and behave. The CBT model for anxiety is:

$$\textbf{Anxiety} = \uparrow\textbf{Risk} + \downarrow\textbf{Resources}$$

This equation means, when we are struggling with anxiety, we perceive our situation as high risk and our resources to respond to the situation as low. Often, when we experience anxiety, we believe our circumstances are worse than they are (high risk). We also think we have no way to change our situation (low resources). I am not referring to dangerous situations but about those moments when we view an event as a higher risk than it is. When we do this, we may have some distortions in our thinking. We will learn to accurately evaluate the risk of a situation and know what resources, both internal and external, are at our disposal.

Step One: Captivate

The first step to change the way we think is to captivate our thoughts. When an anxious thought enters our mind, we need to captivate it and not dwell upon it. The longer we contemplate an anxious idea, the more vulnerable we are to believing it. Scripture encourages us to take every thought captive (2 Corinthians 10:5). What does it look like to take a thought captive? It figuratively means to grab it from your mind and look at it. I think of it as taking the thought in my hand and then observing it. You may want to say the thought out loud. The goal is to become mindful of the thought.

God talks about our thoughts and minds throughout Scripture, indicating he views our thought life as crucial. My prayer is that meditating on a few of the verses below will remind you of the importance of taking our thoughts captive.

- Finally, brothers, whatever is true, whatever is noble, whatever is right, whatever is pure, whatever is lovely, whatever is admirable—if anything is excellent or praiseworthy—think about such things. — Philippians 4:8
- A simple man believes anything, but a prudent man gives thought to his steps. — Proverbs 14:15
- A wicked man puts up a bold front, but an upright man gives thought to his ways. — Proverbs 21:29

You can also look up the following verses on our thought life: 2 Peter 3:1, Romans 8:6, Jeremiah 17:10, and Matthew 22:37.

When I find my mind wandering to anxious thoughts, I often quote Philippians 4:8 to remind myself of what I need to focus my thinking on.

Pastor Rick Warren says one of the key ingredients to lasting change requires us to think in new ways. He wrote: "The way you think determines the way you feel and the way you feel determines the way you act. If you want to change how you act, you must begin by changing the way you think. Your thoughts are the autopilot of your life."[24] He then quotes Romans 12:2. "Don't copy the behavior and customs of this world but let God transform you into a new person by changing the way you think. Then you will learn to know God's will for you, which is good and pleasing and perfect" (NLT).

Keeping in mind that our thoughts determine our emotions and our behavior, we need to identify the thoughts behind our feelings of anxiety. You can ask yourself, *What went through my mind when such-and-such happened?* The following diagram might help you determine your thoughts and feelings about a situation.

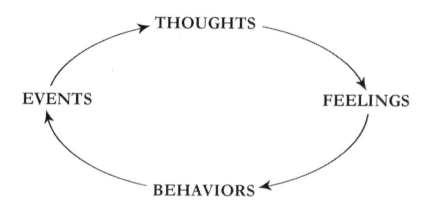

Events are external or internal situations. External events are all the activities happening around us. An internal event is when a thought pops into our head without necessarily having an external event occur. *Thoughts* are our meaning or interpretation of the event. *Emotions* are the feelings that follow the interpretation of the situation. *Behaviors* are the response to the thoughts of the event.

Let's fill in the blanks from the above diagram using a fictitious scenario that might cause someone anxiety. As you work through these exercises, if you develop significant anxiety, go to Section III, and apply the relaxation techniques that work best for you.

Suppose you are at a gathering where you don't know many people. You see a friend, and you walk toward her, hoping to connect with her and sit at the same table. As you approach her, she turns away and takes the last seat at a crowded table. She doesn't acknowledge you. She just looks in the other direction.

1. Fill in the event using the above scenario (I did it for you).

Event:
   You are at a gathering where your friend turns away and sits at a now full table.

2. Fill in what thoughts crossed your mind when you read the scenario.

Thoughts:

_____

_____

_____

3. Fill in the emotion. For this scenario and our purposes, it is anxiety. If you would experience more than anxiety, write what other feelings you may have.

Emotion: <u>Anxiety</u>

4. Fill in the behaviors you might have as a result of the thoughts you mentioned.

Behaviors:

_____

_____

_____

Let's go over the diagram together. We have already filled in part one, the event. For part two, everyone's thoughts or interpretation of the event will be different. There is no wrong answer. I will use my friend Lori's responses: "Oh no, she must not like me anymore. What did I do wrong? I am such a bad person."

For category three, the emotion is anxiety. For the fourth component, ask yourself, "How might I respond to my thoughts?" Again, there are many possible answers to this question, none of which are wrong. Lori said, "I might stress out the entire gathering and sleep little that night. I might cry about it and leave the party. When I get home, I might eat a pint of ice cream and ruminate over what I might have done wrong."

Step 2: Evaluate

Now that we have filled out the four categories of the model, we need to ask some questions about the thoughts we have captivated. This is Step 2 in changing how we think. First, we captivate our thoughts, and then we evaluate them. Here are some questions to ask yourself about the thoughts or the meaning you placed on the event.

- Do I think this event is a higher risk than it is?
- Do I have any resources that might help me respond to my situation?
- Could my thoughts be inaccurate?
- Can I create other thoughts that would make more sense?
- Are any of my thoughts distorted?

We must understand that just because we believe a thought to be true doesn't mean it is. Anxious thoughts are almost always inaccurate. Never elevate feelings above truth. First John 1:8 says, "If we claim to be without sin, we deceive ourselves and the truth is not in us." We can deceive ourselves with our thoughts. Distorted thinking is a common occurrence in our lives, especially when we are feeling anxious. The good news is, as we develop more-rational thinking, our anxiety will decrease.

Below is a list of common cognitive distortions that will be extremely helpful to learn and understand. Determining the cognitive distortions we tend to use will help us think differently, and therefore, reduce anxiety.

Common Cognitive Distortions:

- 1. **<u>Jumping to Conclusions</u>**: Predicting something will go a certain way before it happens. There are two ways of doing this: One is by Mind Reading, assuming we know what someone is thinking or feeling. Example: Nick is eating alone in a restaurant, and he assumes people think he is a loser because he is by himself. The second is Fortune Telling: Predicting things will turn out badly without any evidence. Example: Beth's husband is late, so she assumes he is having an affair.

- 2. **<u>Shoulds</u>:** We believe people and situations *should* or *shouldn't* be a certain way. Shoulds can include *musts* and *have-tos*. Shoulds are a form of legalism. Example: Shelly believes she should read her Bible for at least an hour every day.

- 3. **<u>Catastrophizing</u>:** We think the worst-case scenario will occur. Example: The plane you are in hits turbulence. You assume the aircraft is going down, and everyone will die.

- 4. **<u>Overgeneralizing</u>**: We make a generalized conclusion based on one event. Example: "I always hit every red light on my way home."

- 5. **<u>Labeling</u>**: Applying labels to ourselves or others. Labeling can blind us to other qualities in ourselves and others. Example: If we or someone else makes a mistake, we say something like, "I am such an idiot," or "He is such a loser."

- **6. Personalizing**: We hold ourselves responsible for things that may not have been our fault. Personalization is common in children who have been mistreated. Example: Children who are treated poorly tend to assume they are to blame and therefore will see themselves as defective. Adult example: Kathy is beaten by her boyfriend, and she blames herself for the abuse.

- **7. Blaming**: When the cognitive distortion of personalizing is reversed, we have blaming. We blame others for a situation we took part in creating. Example: George was fired, because he was late ten times. Instead of taking responsibility for being fired, he blames his boss for being a poor manager of his employees.

- **8. Polarizing/All or Nothing**: We see situations as either perfect or a complete failure. There is no middle ground. Example: Johnny catches two fly balls, gets three hits, and strikes out once. He considers his game and himself a failure.

- **9. Filtering**: We only see the negative aspects of a situation while screening out the positive issues. Filtering looks similar to polarizing, but how we get to the negative conclusions is different. Example: After Sue's yearly work review, she only focuses on her boss's one critical comment while ignoring all the compliments she received.

- **10. Emotional Reasoning**: We assume how we feel is an accurate reflection of how things are. Example: Malorie is feeling anxious, so she assumes that something terrible is going to happen.

Now go back and look at our example. Lori said, "Oh no, she must not like me anymore. What did I do wrong? I am such a bad person." Was anything distorted about her thinking? Look at the list of cognitive distortions above and see if any fit.

- She must not like me anymore. Mind reading.
- What did I do wrong? Personalizing.
- I am such a loser. Labeling.

Try this with the thoughts you wrote down in the scenario about the woman whose friend ignored her.

Let's try another one. This time write down any cognitive distortions that might be present.

One evening when my son Drew was sixteen, he was late for curfew. I became extremely anxious. My first thought was, *He hasn't called. What if he has been killed or seriously injured in an accident?* Anxious thoughts often come with vivid images. I am not only *thinking* about the horrible words, but I am also *picturing* the event happening, increasing my anxiety.

My reactions to my thoughts were: I called Drew, but there was no answer. I woke my husband, crying and sharing my fears. When I was about to call my son's friends, he walked in. I screamed at him and grounded him for a year.

Let's get a visual of the process that is occurring.

- Event: Son is late for curfew.
- Thoughts: He has been in an accident and maybe seriously injured or killed.
- Feeling: Anxiety.
- Behaviors: Call, son. Wake husband, crying. Scream and ground son.

What cognitive distortion(s) do you see? Don't look below until you have tried to fill in your ideas.

What distortions fit these thoughts?

What if he has been in an accident? Fortune Telling (which is part of Jumping to Conclusions).

What if he is dead? Catastrophizing.

If you got it right, good for you. If you didn't, that's okay, because it takes practice. Fortune telling is a common cognitive distortion. I am a master of it. James addresses this issue when he says, "We don't even know what will happen tomorrow" (James 4:14). How unreasonable is thinking ahead and believing we know everything that has happened or can predict what will happen?

Let's practice again.

Recall a recent time when you felt anxious. Using the space below or a separate piece of paper, write what happened.

Event:

_____

_____

_____

Try to recall what went through your mind when you were in that anxiety-provoking situation. Write those thoughts. You can also ask yourself, *What did the situation mean to me?* If you had more than one thought, write them all.

Thoughts:

_____

_____

_____

Write the emotion that went with your thoughts. We can have more than one emotion in a given situation, so feel free to write any other feelings you experienced during your event.

46

Feeling:

_____

_____

_____

Write how you responded to your thoughts about the event.

Behavior:

_____

_____

_____

After you have filled in the four parts, look at the list of cognitive distortions and write any that fit your thoughts. If you do not believe there were any distortions, you might want to ask a trusted friend for a second opinion. Denial is common in cognitive distortions.

Cognitive Distortions:

_____

_____

_____

If you don't see any distortions or you believe you can justify a distortion, the following exercise might help. It's called Reviewing the Evidence. We are looking at the validity of our thoughts—a reality check

The steps to Reviewing the Evidence are:

- Identify your thought.
- To what degree do you believe this thought to be accurate? Assign a percentage from 0 to 100.
- On a sheet of paper, write all the evidence you can come up with that indicates your thought(s) are correct.

- On another sheet, write all the evidence that indicates your thought(s) are false.
- At this point, in light of the new evidence, you may want to reevaluate the degree to which you believe your thought is accurate. If the percentage has changed, write it down.
- If you find there is more evidence for the thought being true, go with it.
- On the other hand, if you find more evidence that your thought is false, consider possible alternative thoughts to your situation.

Let's look at the example of my son being late for curfew.

Below is what Reviewing the Evidence would look like:

- Identified Thought: My son is late, has been in a horrible car accident, and is seriously injured or dead.
- Degree of Belief: 70 percent.
- Evidence for Thought: I sometimes hear about teenagers dying behind the wheel of a car. He has been driving for less than a year.
- Evidence against Thought: My son has never been in an accident. He can lose track of time when playing video games with his friends. He often forgets to charge his phone. He has been late before and has had a reasonable excuse. I tend to catastrophize and jump to conclusions.
- Reevaluated Degree of Belief: 15 percent.
- With more evidence that my son has not been in a car accident and is seriously injured, I want to consider an alternative thought pattern.

Having no distortions is possible for some thoughts that produce anxiety, but dissecting them is imperative if there are any.

Another way to evaluate our thoughts is to use Philippians 4:8 as a reference point. God tells us to think upon whatever is true, noble, right, pure, lovely, admirable, excellent, or praiseworthy. If what we are thinking is not on the list, it's probably not worth thinking about. If you are experiencing anxiety, ask if your thoughts are consistent with at least one of the above traits. This verse is an excellent guide to determine if our thinking is off.

Step 3: Renovate

After we have analyzed our thoughts, we need to renovate any distortions and come up with alternative perspectives that are more probable and realistic. The best way to find alternative thoughts to explain our situation is to brainstorm. Write anything that comes to mind. Renovating or replacing our anxious thoughts is much more effective than trying to erase or avoid them. Avoiding anxiety increases anxiety. Trying to erase fearful thoughts leaves a void where other anxious thoughts will vie for our attention.

Looking at my previous example about my son being late might help. I have determined that my son is forty-five minutes late, and I feel a significant amount of anxiety. I think he has been in a car accident and might be seriously injured. I am picturing a terrible crash. I have determined that my thought patterns for this situation are flawed. I am jumping to conclusions and catastrophizing the event. I take three slow, deep breaths and use muscle relaxation to stay calm and to stimulate my pre-frontal cortex, which will allow me to effectively brainstorm any other reasons my son might be late.

We are encouraged in Scripture to be "transformed by the renewing" of our minds (Romans 12:2). Colossians 3:2 tells us to set our minds "on things above, not on earthly things." We are encouraged to have "wholesome thinking" (2 Peter 3:1) and "whatever is true, whatever is noble, whatever is right, whatever is pure, whatever is lovely, whatever is admirable—if anything is excellent or praiseworthy—think about such things" (Philippians

4:8). When we think of such things, we will experience less anxiety. Remember, the thoughts we think most will be the strongest.

As I renew my mind regarding my son being late, I brainstorm more realistic alternative thoughts. Below are some ideas.

Alternative Thoughts:

- Maybe he was hungry and stopped by a drive-thru to get something to eat.
- Maybe he was having so much fun with his friends playing a video game, he lost track of time.
- Maybe he didn't hear his phone ring, because he left it in his car or the battery died.

As you come up with alternative thoughts, replace the negative images with positive ones. I imagined my son playing video games with his friends. I then saw him going through his favorite drive-thru to get food. After you brainstorm, think about the evidence for each alternative thought. Coming up with *evidence* for our thoughts helps us keep distortions at bay. Then ask yourself if the alternative thoughts are more probable or realistic.

For example,

Evidence for Alternative Thoughts:

- My son is always hungry and likes to pick up food to eat before he goes to bed.
- He quickly loses track of time when he is playing video games.
- I may also remember that he sometimes forgets to charge his phone.

As we calm our feelings of anxiety and our thinking brain is activated, we may be more able to develop other responses. For me, I could use my find-the-phone app to locate my son's phone, or I could wait another ten or fifteen minutes and call a few of his friends who might be with him. Before the ten minutes is up, my son walks in the door. He was with David, playing Fortnite, and his phone had died. He hadn't considered using his friend's phone to call. I then grounded him for a week.

Once you develop alternative thoughts that are more realistic and lessen your anxiety, you may still have the old anxious thoughts pop into your mind. This is normal. Be intentional to think, *I have come up with alternative thoughts about this situation, and I am believing them until I get evidence to disprove my new, more calming ideas.*

Practicing these exercises while you are calm is very important. Practice them again and again. As you practice these techniques *before* an anxiety-provoking situation occurs, you will get better at staying calm. That's because you have already thought of alternative cognitive responses to your circumstances. Practice your deep breathing. Practice the other exercises, such as meditation and mindfulness (see Section III). Of course, you need to be exercising regularly and eating healthily (see Section IV).

Half the equation to anxiety is believing our situation is a higher risk than it is. The other half is assuming we have fewer resources than we actually have. Even though we have internal and external resources, we don't always believe we can handle a situation. The key is knowing what those resources are. We have varying internal strengths. Some of us are patient. Others are courageous. We might be street smart, book smart, a good problem solver, or physically strong. The list is endless.

In addition to internal strengths, we have external resources. On the Internet, we can learn just about anything. We have family and friends to guide us. The Word of God is there to give us wisdom. Counselors, professionals, and thousands of great books are available to help in all areas. Apart from Scripture, one of the most valuable resources we can have is being part of a church family. The Word of God tells us, "Praise be to the God and Father of our Lord Jesus

Christ, the Father of compassion and the God of all comfort, who comforts us in all our troubles so that we can comfort those in any trouble with the comfort we ourselves have received from God" (2 Corinthians 1:3–4). We have a resource in our Triune God and the body of believers. Take an inventory of your internal and external resources. Write them on notecards and place them around the house. You have more than you think. If you need help, ask a trusted friend, a pastor, or a counselor.

Application:

Well done! You have completed plenty of application in this chapter. Keep practicing these techniques.

Questions:

1. What was your favorite exercise in this chapter? Why?

2. What was your least favorite exercise? Why? Discuss your answers with someone or journal about your experience.

CHAPTER 5
WHY DO WE THINK
THE WAY WE DO?

Fear doesn't exist anywhere except the mind.
— Dale Carnegie

When my husband, Patrick, and I were first married and we argued, my husband would leave the house. He was only gone for twenty minutes, but I freaked out. I thought we were on the brink of divorce. When he returned, I cried and said, "How dare you leave me like that." He responded with, "I left so I wouldn't say something I would regret." After several painful arguments, I realized that his leaving was triggering something deep inside me.

You see, when I was a child and my mom and dad argued, my dad would leave too. However, he was gone for days, weeks, or even months at a time. My parents separated several times during my childhood and divorced when I was sixteen.*

I connected my husband's leaving with the painful memories of my dad *abandoning* me. The reality is, our life experiences have a significant impact on how we think. Our past can distort the way we think about today. Our past events affect how often we use distorted

---

* My parents remarried several years later.

thinking, what distortions we tend to gravitate toward, and to what degree we use them.

Let's take a moment to understand why we think the way we do. Yes, we are going to talk about our childhoods. For some, this is a difficult topic that might create several emotions, anxiety being one. However, we want to take our thoughts captive and reduce our anxiety, so let's take on the challenge. If you experience a significant amount of anxiety, use the relaxation techniques that work for you (see Section III).

Core Beliefs

Sometimes the bad things that happen in our lives put us directly on the path to the most wonderful things that will ever happen to us.
— *Nicole Reed*

So why do we think the way we do? Why do I go straight to *My son is late, so he must have been in a car accident?* Instead of thinking, like my husband: *My son is late because he is a teenage boy and loses track of time and wants to push every limit we set.* The answer is core beliefs. Our core beliefs have a significant impact on our automatic thoughts.

Automatic thoughts are those thoughts that pop into our heads without pondering the situation. Automatic thoughts come from our subconscious mind. These thoughts get to our subconscious mind by being a part of our conscious mind enough times to become part of who we are, deeply wired into our brains. We need to understand that our subconscious mind is much more powerful than our conscious mind, which is why we have to work so hard to change our automatic thoughts. When we repeatedly rehearse and focus on a thought, it moves from the conscious to the subconscious mind.

The analogy of a tree might be helpful. The conscious mind is the parts of the tree we see above the ground—the trunk, branches, and leaves representing our thoughts and images that produce words and behaviors. The subconscious mind is like the roots that are continually nourishing and supporting the tree. Once thoughts are in the subconscious mind, they begin to feed the conscious mind.

Our thoughts are based on our core beliefs, and our core beliefs are based on our life experiences. How we responded to our life experiences as children become deeply wired into our brains. Therefore, these responses, or neuropathways, become automatic responses.

Core beliefs are founded on what we believe about ourselves, others, life, and God. We usually hold firmly to our core beliefs, but that doesn't mean they are always accurate or beneficial. We must examine and challenge the core beliefs that are not in our best interest. As we understand our core beliefs, we will know why we have the thoughts we have. When we have automatic ideas that are irrational and destructive, they usually come from core beliefs that are also irrational and destructive. As we change the core beliefs that are destructive and create more-realistic and accurate ones, our thoughts will also evolve and become less distorted. The more realistic our thoughts are, the less anxiety we will experience. Let me say that again: the more accurate our thoughts, the less anxiety we will experience.

One way to get to our core beliefs is to ask ourselves some real-life questions. Below are just a few that might be helpful.

- What did I hear a lot growing up?
- How do I view myself and others?
- What did I learn to be sensitive to (mother's criticism, dad's inability to listen)?
- What was the message I received about sexuality?
- What did I believe about God as a child, as well as what do I believe now?
- Do I see God more as a judge or as a loving Father?

- What are my thoughts about trust, goodness, life, and death?
- What did I need most that I didn't receive from my parents?

Ponder the questions that touch something in you. Identifying your core beliefs takes time, so be patient with yourself. As you work through this process, you will find some of your core beliefs will stay the same, some will radically change, some will be modified, and still others will be completely new. Below are a few examples of core beliefs.

- I am unlovable.
- I am loved.
- I am stupid.
- Life is scary.
- People will hurt me.
- God is love.
- People are usually safe.
- God is angry with me.
- I am not good enough.
- If I make a mistake, I will be rejected.
- I cannot trust anyone.
- No one sees me.
- I am disgusting.
- I am forgiven.

Retired Navy SEAL Eric Greitens talks about our philosophies in his book *Resilience: Hard Won Wisdom for Living a Better Life*. He uses the term *philosophies* as I use the term *core beliefs*. Read what he has to say about this topic: "We learn a lot about the philosophies we're living if we spell them out. Ridiculous philosophies, dishonest philosophies, destructive philosophies have their tightest hold on us when they're invisible. Then there are philosophies that work, produce what they're supposed to produce: real happiness. Thoreau said that the best philosophies 'solve some of the problems of life, not only theoretically, but practically.' We can tell a philosophy is working; he said if it produces 'a life of simplicity, independence, magnanimity, and trust.' The question is, are you aware of the philosophy you have —assumptions, beliefs, and ideas add up to shape your life? Can they stand exposure to the light of day?"[25]

These are great questions. As you examine your core beliefs and expose them to the light of day, determine if they produce the spiritual, mental, and physical health you desire.

We all leave our childhoods with emotional wounds. If you think you might be the exception, you not only have childhood wounds, but you may also be in denial. I say that with lots of love. It is essential to understand that the wounds we receive in childhood are filtered through a child's mind, which creates a worldview that goes with us into adulthood. Think about that. Our core beliefs from our childhood experiences become a part of our adult life and significantly affect how we think and act. Doesn't it make sense that we examine these beliefs with the filter of our adult minds? Not doing this is like having a twenty-year-old computer and never upgrading the software. Consider what 1 Corinthians 13:11 says: "When I was a child, I talked like a child. I reasoned like a child. When I became a man, I put childish ways behind me." One of the great benefits of growing older is the wisdom that comes with age. Use your knowledge to grow and mature your heart and mind.

When you were a child, you had some challenging life experiences, and you developed coping strategies to deal with those experiences. For some, these challenges happened regularly (abuse, abrasive words, too high of expectations, neglect). As we responded to these experiences, we developed coping skills that were limited and childlike. As children, we don't have many options to cope with being wounded, especially traumatic wounds. So we respond to these experiences to fit our temperaments, which helps us protect our hearts and possibly even survive. One common way children cope is by being *good.* These kids think, *If I'm good enough, my parent won't do that again,* or *My friends won't tease me.* Another frequent coping response with kids is being rebellious and angry. *If I am mean or show rage, people will keep their distance.* Withdrawing is another coping skill many children use. *If I stay invisible, no one will notice me, and therefore, they won't hurt me.* Many of us coped with life by becoming anxious. *If I worry about what might happen, I won't be as disappointed or scared when it does.* Of course, there are many other coping skills we develop as children. What did you do?

The reality is, our childhood wounds are triggered in adulthood. This triggering causes us to revert to our childhood coping style. Think about the last time you argued with a loved one. How did you respond? Did you withdraw? Did you become angry and lash out? Did you play the martyr? Many times we do what we did when there was a conflict in our childhood homes. Sometimes we do the opposite. For example, if there was a great deal of arguing in your childhood home and you hid in your bedroom, your response to a conflict as an adult might be to withdraw. Or you might become combative because you have decided you won't be intimidated like you were as a child.

Even with all the work I have done, I sometimes revert to withdrawing. A few years ago, I became angry with my teenage son and stomped off. The next day I was still reticent with him. He said to me, "Are you still not talking to me? That is so immature." Yikes, he was right. I must fight my childhood coping style.

One other issue I want to mention is that we can develop a high tolerance for others' wounding behaviors. For instance, if you had an abusive father, you may tolerate an abusive boyfriend, husband, or friend. Many of us, when we see this in someone, we are astounded. However, we are all vulnerable to this, because we tend to relive our pasts in some form—another reason we need to upgrade our mental software.

The good news is that we can learn new, more adult-like coping skills. Learning to respond to stressors with upgraded more-adult-like behavior will allow us to feel more empowered, reinforcing more change.

Application:

Write any core beliefs you are aware of, and think about where they came from.

_____

_____

_____

Questions:

1. What was it like to think about challenging childhood experiences? What emotions came up?

_____

_____

_____

2. What childhood experience came up? Talk with someone about your experience or journal about it.

_____

_____

_____

CHAPTER 6
DETERMINING OUR CORE BELIEFS

All people cross the line from childhood to
adulthood with a secondhand opinion of who
they are without questioning. We take as truth
whatever our parents and other influential
people have said about us during our childhood.
Whether these messages are communicated
verbally, physically, or silently.
—Hayward Bruce Ewart III

Oh no, not again. During P.E., why do we always have to play dodgeball? I hate dodgeball.

The teacher tells us to get into a line. She picks two captains, one for each team. She tells them to choose their teams, one junior high classmate at a time. I begin to sweat. I'm thinking, *Please don't get picked last. Can there be just one time where I can be picked second-to-last?*

I hear all my classmate's names being called, one after another. We are down to three girls and one boy. My heart is racing, and I just want to hide behind the module. Can't the teacher see how mortifying this is for those of us still standing in line? Joey is called. Then I hear Lisa's name. There are two of us left. I pray. I hear my friend Kamii's name called. *Shoot.* The captain, who now has to pick me, says to the other captain, "You can have her too."

I'm crushed. But the worst is yet to come. I still have to play this stupid game. I try to find the biggest kid I can to hide behind. As I am running, I am hit with the big, red dodge ball in the back of my legs. I fall to the ground, scraping my knees. I'm bleeding, but the hurt I feel on the inside is much worse than the pain I feel on my knees. I feel like the worst of all losers.

Identifying our core beliefs can be challenging, because they are not necessarily at the forefront of our minds. Some are deep within our being and come from early childhood experiences we may not even remember. Mind-blowing, isn't it? Others are more obvious. Some are painful, and others bring us joy. Some are incredibly toxic, and others have influenced us to be good people. Some have brought us to the saving knowledge of Jesus Christ, and others have affected our walk with God in a way that has made it challenging to trust him and believe his Word.

Here are a few of my core beliefs to give you an idea of what they look like. I have challenged some of my core beliefs and changed some. There are others that I still battle. Some, I cherish. One core belief of mine is, "I am deeply loved." I knew my entire childhood and into adulthood that my mom loved me. I never questioned it, not even in my teens. This core belief of knowing I am loveable has been such a blessing. Another core belief of mine is, "Bad things are likely to happen in my life." This core belief I revised but still battle with, although to a lesser degree. I believe my tendency to catastrophize is rooted in this belief. The third core belief I want to share, which I developed in my adult years, is: "God works for the good of those who love him, who have been called according to his purpose" (Romans 8:28).

Five days before I had my first son, my brother Darren's son, Dillon, was born with Down's Syndrome. My family was devastated. Three years later, Darren had his second son, Garrett, who was also born with Down's Syndrome. Again, the family grieved. At the time of our grieving, we had no idea the joy and laughter Dillon and Garrett would bring to our lives. They have taught us a great deal over the years: what pure love looks like, how to truly enjoy your birthday, and how to live the present moment in its fullness. Sometimes in our greatest sorrows, we find God's greatest gifts. Indeed God does work all things together for good.

The challenges I have faced have been used by God for his glory. Because of this core belief, I am more able to trust God during hard times. He has used my trials to mold and shape me into his image.

The last core belief I want to share is, "I am uncoordinated." Hence, the story at the beginning of the chapter. I have two brothers and a sister who were all talented athletes. They made the all-star teams in every sport they played. On the other hand, I begged my mom to allow me to skip sports altogether. I played softball for years, and every year I played two innings in right field and never got a hit. My mom coached my soccer team for one year—I think so I could play in a game. I scored a goal, but for the wrong team. My brothers tease me to this day about that.

Several years ago, we had a party for my mom's birthday. My siblings and I got up in front of the large group of partygoers to say something kind about my mom. When my brother, David, got up, he said, "Mom, you were so amazing having four, I mean three and a half athletes and showing up to every game." That was it! I was determined to show my family I could be athletic. I began to run. I started to do triathlons. I began to be an athlete. I even biked across Iowa with my sister, which was 525 miles over seven days. Just a side note: I would never do that again. After the ride, I could not sit down for a week.

I broke the core belief that I was uncoordinated. I confess, I have crashed my bike and ended up in the ER. I have twisted my ankle and cut up my knees. But I can say to myself and my brothers, "I am an athlete."

As I reflect on some of my core beliefs, I am better able to understand why I have certain automatic thoughts that create anxiety. The core belief, "Bad things are likely to happen," reveals itself often in my automatic thoughts. We know bad things happen. Just listen to the news. Horrible things happen every day around the world. However, I tend to maximize the likelihood of bad things happening in my life. Often, my first response to something is to think worst-case scenario. My husband's father died at a young age of a massive heart attack. When my husband and I married, I thought I would probably be a young widow. Every time my husband was sick, I would think he might have a heart attack. I worried about him so much I am surprised I didn't give him a heart attack many years ago. Another one for me was that I would automatically think I had a brain tumor whenever I had a headache. Can anyone relate?

I use many of the techniques we have discussed when I start to feel anxious about my health or the health of a loved one. As we examine our core beliefs, it can be helpful to understand where the beliefs originated. Before we can determine if a core belief is realistic and practical or false and destructive, we have to know what our core belief is.

I had to think about why I believed bad things are likely to happen. At first, I wasn't sure why I felt this so strongly. Then I remembered my youth when our next-door neighbors were killed in a car accident. What a tragedy. Five kids were left without parents. It shook my world. A few years later, my brothers' best friend's dad died of a heart attack. The boy was ten years old, left without a father. He stayed with us a great deal during that time, and I remember his incredible grief. Bad things do happen, and if we cannot talk about them and understand them, especially as children, the trauma can distort our thinking and become bigger than life.

Vertical Arrow Technique

Determining our core beliefs takes time and patience. Give yourself grace as you work through this process. Dr. David Burns talks about a technique I found helpful as I began to explore my core beliefs. He calls it the Vertical Arrow Technique in his *Feeling Good Handbook*.[26]

As we dissect our automatic thoughts, it is helpful to try and decipher what the core beliefs are behind those thoughts. In the Vertical Arrow Technique, we go along with the negative thinking to see where it leads us, usually leading us to the core belief behind it. First, write down your automatic thought and then place an arrow (>)next to it. Each > represents the question: *If that thought were true, why would it be upsetting to me?* This question will lead to another negative thought and another. Each time you answer the question, write it down, and make another > to represent the question: *If that thought were true, why would it be upsetting to me?* Keep going with this thought process until you have exhausted the line of questioning. After you have generated as many thoughts as you can and you keep getting the same answer, evaluate the negative thoughts and ask yourself, *What do these negative thoughts tell me about my value system? What are my underlying assumptions about myself or others?*

Let me give you a model. Replace the > with the question, "If this thought were true, why would it be upsetting to me?" Here is a simplified example: the automatic thought is:

> (1) If my daughter doesn't get straight A's, she won't go to a good college.

> (2) If she doesn't go to a good college, I haven't raised her well.

> (3) If I didn't raise her well, I am a bad mother.

> (4) If I am a bad mother, I will be rejected by everyone.

The core belief here is, "My worth and acceptance are based on my kids' performance." Let's do that again. I will use an example a friend of mine worked through. Her friend had cancer, and she was feeling very anxious about it. The automatic thought was, *I am so afraid because my friend has cancer.* Then I asked her, "If this thought were true, why would it be so upsetting to you?" The answer to the question, or the next automatic thought, was that she would *get sick and die.*

> I would feel depressed.

> When feeling depressed, I wouldn't want to do anything.

> I would be boring to others.

> People wouldn't love me.

The core belief for this automatic thought is, *People won't love me if I feel sadness.* You will find after you do this with several automatic thoughts, you will begin to notice a pattern. There will be a theme in your beliefs (for example, people won't accept me).

When you become aware of one of your core beliefs, write it down and ask if it is a healthy, realistic belief or an inaccurate and destructive one. Does this statement, "If I feel sadness, people won't love me," sound accurate? Does it seem constructive? Is this core belief healthy and beneficial? Can you come up with examples in your life where this is not true? In the previous example, the core belief was, "My worth and acceptance are based on my child's performance." You can ask yourself, *Is my child's performance a true reflection of my worth? Is it possible she is her own person, and straight A's are not her top priority? Is she even capable of getting straight A's? Is this vital in the scheme of things? Will this matter in ten years? Do I need to challenge this core belief?*

Advantages and Disadvantages of Core Beliefs

If you are not sure if you need to give up or change a core belief, it can help to write out your core belief's advantages and disadvantages. List the benefits on the left side of a piece of paper and the difficulties on the right side. Here is an example of going through the advantages and disadvantages of my core belief, "Bad things are likely to happen."

Advantages	Disadvantages
• I'm prepared for the worst.	• I'm never in the present moment.
• I won't be so surprised when it happens.	• I'm hurting my body worrying all the time.
	• I hurt my relationships by being negative.
	• I create an anxious environment for my kids.
	• It's hard to have the joy of the Lord.

I could probably come up with more disadvantages, but you get my point. I can see this is not a core belief I need to keep.

On the following page, you will find a worksheet you can use to write the advantages and disadvantages of each of the core beliefs you identify. Make copies of the worksheet so you can complete it each time you recognize one of your core beliefs.

Analyzing the Effects of a Core Belief

Identified Core Belief:

_____

_____

_____

_____

_____

ADVANTAGES OF HOLDING THIS BELIEF	DISADVANTAGES OF HOLDING THIS BELIEF

Revised Core Belief:

_____

_____

After you look at the advantages and disadvantages of the core belief and find more disadvantages, ask yourself, *Would I benefit from revising this core belief to make it more realistic or healthy?* If you are going to make changes, writing the alternative belief is essential. For example, the core belief that I assumed terrible things were likely to happen was not helping me, and it was inaccurate. I cognitively revised how I viewed future life events. I didn't have to assume that something terrible was going to happen. My revised or alternative core belief is, "Bad things happen on this earth, but more good things happen, and all things work together for my good because I love God." Worrying about the future doesn't change the future. It only hurts my mind and body.

Whenever I have automatic thoughts about this previous core belief, I remember the decision to change it. Because I wrote my core belief, I can go to my journal and repeatedly reread the new version. Ephesians 4:22–24 tells us to put off the old and put on the new. We need to replace old thought patterns with new ones. If we get rid of a core belief and don't replace it with a new, healthier one, there will be a void that can make it easier for the old thoughts to blindside us. Taking every thought captive is a day-to-day, moment-by-moment, repeated choice and action.

We must keep practicing healthy thinking. Be patient with yourself. Changing core beliefs is challenging. Permit yourself to work through this process over time. We need to fight our old patterns to create new ones.

Application:

You have completed plenty of applications for this chapter. Well done.

Questions:

1. What was your experience exploring your core beliefs?

_____

_____

_____

2. Did you determine any core beliefs that needed to be modified or replaced? If so, do you feel relief or concern by the changes?

_____

_____

_____

CHAPTER 7
MEMORY

Sometimes I get anxiety because I don't feel anxious. Which means I forgot what I was supposed to be anxious about in the first place, and that gives me anxiety. — Nanea Hoffman

I'm babysitting two little girls, and they are fast asleep. I am fourteen years old, and my friends had just seen the 1979 version of *When a Stranger Calls*. I refused to see the movie, because I hate scary movies. However, my girlfriends hadn't stopped talking about the film and how frightening it was. While I babysat, I kept remembering what my friends had said about the killer in the movie. He had called the babysitter from inside the house, threatening to kill her and the children.

I thought I heard a noise upstairs, where the girls were sleeping. I was so scared, I could hardly breathe. Paralyzed with fear, I called my mom and told her I thought someone was in the house and to hurry over. Of course, there was no killer in the house. My mom knew me well enough to know my imagination had gotten the best of me. I didn't babysit for months after that fear-filled evening.

A great book I read during my research on anxiety was *Anatomy of the Soul* by Dr. Curt Thompson. He does a great job on the issue of neuroscience and spiritual practices. He encourages his readers by saying we can change the way we remember our past. He states, "No matter how fixed your thinking or behavior is, research tells us you can make significant changes in the way you remember your past. The way you experience the way your parents treated you . . . In other words, even though you cannot change the events of your story, you can change the way you experience your story."[27] So how do we experience our past or interpret it differently? One way is to restructure the meaning of early experiences. Another way to say this is to reframe our childhood memories using our *adult* minds.

For example, I grew up with an alcoholic father. As a child, I thought if I was a good girl I could make my dad stop drinking and make him come home more. My child's brain thought I had some control over my dad's drinking. That was not true. In no way is a child responsible for a parent's inappropriate behavior. In my experience of my father's drinking, I blamed myself. As I grew older, I had to ask myself, *Were there other possible explanations for my dad's behavior?* I was able to come up with various theories and test them. First, I realized that my dad drank because he was an alcoholic, and no matter how I behaved, he would drink. This was confirmed because he continued to drink after I moved out. Another theory I came up with was, my dad drank because he was broken due to his own parents' alcoholism. Both of these theories are possible and probable. I was able to talk with my dad about his drinking. He is currently sober, and he reassured me that his drinking was not about me or anyone else, but rather it was 100 percent about him. Therefore, by restructuring my thought pattern about my father's alcoholism, I could experience my past differently. By doing this, I forgave my dad and mended our relationship. And most importantly, I no longer bear any burden for my dad's drinking. We have become very close, and I have enjoyed watching him be an available grandfather to my boys.

I realize that many of your stories are much more traumatic than what I went through. Many of you will not have the opportunity to mend your relationships as I have. I encourage you to look at your past and see if you can find new ways to understand some of your painful experiences. I am in no way saying to discount those events. Instead, I am asking, Can you find ways to rethink them? If your mom was abusive or a drug addict, or your grandfather molested you, and you think somehow you deserved that treatment or were in some way responsible for their behavior, ask yourself, *Is it possible that the way I was treated had nothing to do with me. Could the person who hurt me have been sick, broken, or maybe just plain evil?* If you did not cause it, then you are not responsible for it.

As I mentioned earlier, my father-in-law died of a heart attack when my husband was eleven years old. Patrick is the youngest of eight children, and they were all on a ski vacation when their father, who was only fifty-one, collapsed on the ski slope. After they brought him down the mountain, Patrick ran to wrap his arms around his daddy. His life changed forever that day. He didn't think it was his fault that his dad died, but he hated God for allowing his dad to die. He carried that hatred for a long time. Patrick couldn't understand how God wanted his dad in Heaven more than Patrick needed his dad on Earth. Unfortunately, he carried that hate into his teen and young adult years by using drugs and making terrible choices. What Patrick needed was to process his trauma and his loss. Of course, even if he could have processed his loss at that time, he still would have deeply grieved his father and may have still gone through some rough spots in adolescence. Also, for an eleven-year-old to *rethink* his loss would be challenging. However, when our minds become fully developed and mature emotionally and psychologically, we can review our past experiences. That's what Patrick had to do to become more loving and compassionate. It took a great deal of hard work. Now, instead of seeing his father's death as a *mean thing* God did, he can see his father's death as a tragedy in his life, one that was a part of a tapestry of God's grace, love, and redemption.

You might ask, "What did the hard work consist of?" It took years of meditating on God's Word to know God intimately, memorizing verses that described who he is and who Patrick is in his sight. It took going through the grieving process with a counselor and telling his story again and again. Letting go of his anger toward God and rethinking his experience was a large part of his healing. After Patrick read the above paragraph, he wanted me to add that having a compassionate, loving, *amazing* wife, who happens to be a psychologist, helped (I added the amazing part).

In his book, *Brainstorm: The Power and Purpose of the Teenage Brain*, Dr. Daniel Siegel perfectly states what I am trying to say: "The research is quite clear. When we make sense of events in our lives that made no sense, the mind can become coherent, our relationships more fulfilling, and our brains function in a more integrated way."[28]

Victor Frankl was an Austrian neurologist, psychiatrist, and Holocaust survivor who wrote one of my all-time favorite books, *Man's Search for Meaning*, which chronicles his experiences as a concentration-camp inmate. His experience led him to discover the importance of finding meaning in all circumstances. Frankl believed that even in suffering the worst conditions, we can still choose how we respond to the experience. We can find meaning in every situation. Frankl wrote: "It is a question of the attitude one takes toward life's challenges and opportunities, both large and small. A positive attitude enables a person to endure suffering and disappointment as well as enhance enjoyment and satisfaction. A negative attitude intensifies pain and deepens disappointments. It undermines and diminishes pleasure, happiness, and satisfaction. It may even lead to depression or physical illness."[29]

Implicit vs. Explicit Memory

Sometimes you will never know the value of a
moment until it becomes a memory.
—Dr. Seuss

There are two kinds of memory, implicit and explicit. Implicit memories are implied, not explicitly recalled. The ability to integrate implicit memories in our brain is present at birth. It is what we encode in our minds during subconscious learning and experiences. For example, as infants, we do not encode experiences we can remember specifically. However, we will integrate the emotions, the touch, the bonding, the care we receive, which will attach to our brain's limbic system (emotional center), and those experiences become implicit memories. Often, we think infants and young children don't remember what happened to them, but that is not true. They may not recall specific events, but they will have a recollection that they were loved nor not loved. For instance, a baby who wasn't fed when he was hungry will not remember being hungry, but he will have an emotional response that he didn't get his needs met when he cried. If the neglect continued, he might not develop an attachment with his caretaker, which in turn will affect the rest of his life.

Here is an example of a woman I worked with who didn't remember a specific event but had an emotional reaction whenever she touched hot water. It wasn't until she approached her mother later in life about her anxiety regarding hot water that her mother told her a story about her stepfather putting her in scolding hot water to punish her as a toddler. The revelation also explained some scarring she had. She didn't remember this horrific experience outright, but she was reacting to this implicit memory's emotional response with a fear of hot water. Even after our explicit memory has developed, traumatic experiences can be encoded in our brains as implicit memories. Sometimes, when we go through something traumatic, our mind, in a sense, shuts down, and our conscious attention turns away from what is happening. Disassociation can be an automatic response that our brains use to allow us to survive a trauma psychologically.

Implicit memories occur throughout our lives, not just in our early years before explicit memories develop. When we experience something we are not paying attention to, that experience can be encoded as an implicit memory. If you drive home from work but don't remember the entire drive, you were on autopilot, using implicit memory to get home.

Another way implicit memory works is when we respond to a situation but are unsure why we responded the way we did. Keep in mind, when we overact in the present, something from our past has usually been triggered. For instance, recall the story I told you about when my husband and I argued and he left. It took me a while to figure out why I would get so worked up when he did this. It was due to my implicit memories of my dad being gone for days. Now, I have explicit memories of my dad leaving, but it was the implicit memory, the emotional memory, that created such an intense reaction. If we don't understand the impact implicit memories have on our response to life, we will struggle in our relationships, our self-awareness, and our mental wellness. "Research in marriage and family therapy suggests that approximately 80 percent of the emotional conflict between couples is rooted in events that predate the couple knowing each other."[30] Implicit memories are potent and can produce emotional responses that we may not understand, because we don't have a *clear* memory to recall.

Explicit memory is much easier to understand as well as to explain. It's what we remember. There are two types of explicit memory. The first is factual memory, when we recall the facts about something (where we live, who was the first U.S. president, what your best friend's name is). The second type of explicit memory is autobiographical, when we recall something we experienced (what we did the night before or what chocolate cake tastes like). Explicit memory develops between eighteen months and two years of age. Even though the ability to form explicit memories occurs by about age two, most people have very few, if any, memories that early. It takes time for neuropathways to develop to create lasting wiring patterns.

Many of our life experiences encode in our brain as memories. These memories create neuropathways in the brain. The more we recall these memories or the more often we have similar experiences, the stronger these neuropathways become. Dr. Curt Thompson says it this way: "When we remember something, we are firing neurons that have been fired before, to a greater or lesser degree of frequency. The more frequently those patterns have been fired, the more easily they will fire in that same pattern in the future. The more we activate the neurons that correlate with a particular experience, the more likely we will be to "recall" or enact that same experience. This is the general way the brain works to create memory."[31] Thompson discusses how this wiring can help us remember birthdays and anniversaries but destructive when our wiring remembers to respond to someone's feeling of anger or disappointment by sulking or yelling. He then makes this profound statement: "This reality shapes our life with Jesus no less than our life with our friends or our teenager."[32] We filter who Jesus is and how we view our relationships through our implicit and explicit memories. If we have never experienced forgiveness or unconditional love, it will be difficult for us to receive those things from God just because we read about them or have heard our pastor talk about them. If we have never received compassion, showing someone else compassion will be challenging. There is no reference for us if there is no mental model for us.

The good news is, there is hope. There is always hope in Christ. We can develop these qualities even if we have never experienced them. We can make new neuropathways by creating unique experiences in our lives. Remember our conversation on neuroplasticity in Chapter 6? Neuroplasticity is the brain's ability to reorganize itself by forming new neural connections. Not only can we create new pathways, but we can also prune the paths we don't need or want anymore.

Our memories significantly impact what creates our fears. Most perceived threats come from what we have experienced or what we have been taught, so our memory is a greater influence than what is happening in the moment. "Our learned history, if it contains trauma, can come forward with such intensity and ferocity that it significantly colors our reality to where we cannot see what is real—for example, that we are perfectly safe almost all of the time. Any time we have an experience that reminds us of the past learning, it can, and often will, come forward with this intensity so that our body responds with arousal as if we are in danger."[33]

Our *learning* of anxiety-producing events has grown immensely due to social media. We hear, read, and watch the news, and that forms at least 90 percent of our perception of the world. Horrific events occur worldwide, and we have access to these events with a simple swipe on our phones. We are bombarded by traumatic events regularly. Much of the time, we choose to look or read, but sometimes it's just in our face. To reduce our anxiety, we must limit the amount of trauma we read and watch. We need to be mindful, not only with the news we observe but with violent TV shows, movies, and books. "Every time we watch something traumatic on a TV series, by reading a novel, or by hearing a story from a friend, our level of traumatic stress is incrementally raised. Eventually, we become traumatized without ever experiencing an event that would be considered traumatic."[34]

Application:

Write any memories you recall that may be contributing to your anxiety.

_____

_____

_____

Questions:

1. What is your response to the idea of remembering your past differently?

_____

_____

_____

2. What life experiences do you have that need to be reevaluated? Write them here.

_____

_____

_____

CHAPTER 8
OTHER COGNITIVE—BEHAVIORAL TECHNIQUES

Nothing, absolutely nothing interrupts anxiety
like gratitude. — Ann Voskamp

I am terrified of sharks. I used to do triathlons and needed to train in the ocean for the event's swim portion. I hated it. For days before the training and especially before race day, I had stomach issues. My husband is an avid swimmer. He swims and surfs in the ocean weekly, even in the winter months (although Southern California doesn't have much of a winter). When I decided to swim in the ocean to participate in triathlons, Patrick was thrilled. He thought he would finally have me as a swim partner, but he was wrong. He swam with me as I hyperventilated and did the backstroke to breathe. One day while swimming, we got into a huge argument about whether there were sharks nearby. He said there weren't any. I insisted there were. My anxiety disconnected my rational thought, and I become a little irrational. I told him he was like a shark and to get me back on land. I only did a few races before realizing I was rapidly aging due to my stress.

There are additional cognitive-behavioral exercises that we can implement in our daily lives to reduce anxiety. These techniques may not get to the core of our anxiety, but they will still help reduce it. They are: facing our anxieties, reframing, thought-stopping, brain teasers, worry time, and keeping a gratitude journal.

Facing Our Anxieties

Avoiding our anxiety increases our anxiety. When we avoid our feelings, we often use destructive means to do so. Alcohol is a common way to avoid emotional pain, especially for those who experience social anxiety. Busyness is a common negative coping mechanism to elude anxiety. Constantly scrolling through social media is another form of destructive behavior. Any addictive behavior is a way to avoid intense emotions.

Another way to avoid anxiety is to run from it. If you are afraid of dogs and stay clear of all dogs, you might avoid going outside or to friends' homes. Avoiding all dogs could leave a void in your life. Remember, avoiding anxiety increases anxiety. When we avoid what creates fear in us, we are telling our brains that we need to be afraid, which teaches the amygdala to respond to the object or situation with even more anxiety.

We need to face our anxieties instead of avoiding them. *Exposure* is a term used in cognitive-behavioral therapy, and it means that to deal with anxiety, we need to walk through the anxiety. We need to expose ourselves to what is creating our anxiety. For example, if you are anxious about spiders, expose yourself to spiders. Before and during the exposure, implementing the relaxation techniques in Section IV is essential. If your fear is too intense for exposure, you will want to work with a trained therapist before implementing this technique.

Eric Greitens said, "Every time we choose to confront our fear, our character evolves and we become more courageous. Every time we choose to love through pain to pursue a purpose larger than ourselves, our character evolves, and we become wiser. Every time we choose to move through suffering, our character evolves, and we become stronger. Over time, through a process of daily choices, we find that we've built courage, strength, and wisdom. We've changed who we are and how we can be of service to the people around us. What choices will you make today?"[35]

As I mentioned before, I am afraid of sharks. I have implemented exposure to the ocean to reduce this fear. I still get scared, but at a level that I occasionally go snorkeling and join my husband paddleboarding when the opportunity arises.

If you fear something that you will probably never have to encounter, I wouldn't stress about it and expose yourself to it. For instance, if you are afraid of skydiving, don't go skydiving. But if you fear driving on the freeway and work thirty miles from home, you may need to work through this fear by exposing yourself to driving on the freeway and boosting your confidence. Facing your anxieties will enable you to know you can be exposed to what you fear and still be okay.

Exposure is best applied in steps. Your level of anxiety about an issue you fear will determine how many steps you need. Below are several steps a person—let's call him Ken—could take if he were moderately afraid to drive on the freeway. If his fear level were high to extremely high, he would need more steps and should possibly work with a trained therapist. Again, the entire time, Ken would be using relaxation techniques.

- Step 1: Sit in his car, imagining he is driving on the freeway.
- Step 2: While driving on side streets, imagine he is on the freeway.
- Step 3: Careful to pick an easy on-ramp when there is little traffic, enter the freeway. Stay in the slow lane until the next off-ramp, then exit the freeway.
- Step 4: Each time he enters the freeway, he stays in the slow lane and goes an additional exit.

- Step 5: As he becomes more comfortable, he moves over a lane and stays on the freeway longer.
- Step 6: After becoming more comfortable with the previous step, he takes other freeways and maybe even moves to the fast lane.

Ken would need to decide what level (0–10) of anxiety the first step creates. He determines that sitting in his car, imagining he is driving produces a Level 4. Ken then practices Step 1 until his anxiety goes down by half, to a Level 2. Then he can move on to Step 2 (while driving on side streets, he imagines he is on the freeway). Before implementing Step 2, Ken must determine how much anxiety Step 2 produces. Step 2 creates a Level 4. Once his Step 2 anxiety goes down by half, in this case to a Level 2, he can move on to Step 3. Ken's anxiety for Step 3 is a Level 7. Therefore, we would need to continue this step until he reaches a 3.5. And on it goes. If Ken's goal is to drive on the freeway with little anxiety, and he chooses to skip ever going into the fast lane, that is okay. Expose yourself enough to reach whatever goal you set for yourself.

Give yourself grace. This process takes time and patience.

Another way we can face our anxieties is to write them down. Writing our fears is more powerful than just thinking about them. Both writing *and* talking about them is even better. When we label our feelings of anxiety, we take the mystery out of them, and they lose some of the power they have over us. That is why journaling is so helpful. Think of this exercise as an anxiety journal. When you feel anxious about something, write it in your journal or the note app on your phone. After you write it down, you can look at it and decide if it is worthy of anxiety. Eric Greitens puts it this way: "You either own your fears or they own you. Fears do their worst work when they knock around in your mind. You can't fight your fears until you put them in front of you. Write your fears down. Make them face you. The minute you do this, your fears will shrink, and you will grow."[36]

82

Reframing

Events do not create anxiety. Our thoughts or interpretations of the events do that. How we interpret an event determines how we will feel about the situation. For example, when I consider the ocean, I think of danger. Sharks live in the ocean, and sharks attack people. My interpretation of the ocean is very negative. When my husband contemplates the ocean, he thinks of fun. There, he can swim, surf, snorkel, and fish. Patrick's interpretation is very positive. The event is the same, but our interpretations are different. The thought of the ocean creates anxiety in me, whereas it creates joy in Patrick.

Reframing helps us create different ways of looking at a situation. I like to use the analogy of looking at a figure through the lens of a camera. At first your camera lens is zoomed way out and you are not sure what you are looking at. It could be a large animal, which creates fear in you. As you zoom in, you see the figure is a person, and you feel some relief. You zoom in some more, and you see the person is a woman. She looks like she might be crying, which leaves you feeling sad. You zoom in again and see the woman isn't crying. She is laughing hysterically, and you smile and feel happiness. The figure is the same, no matter what focal point you are observing, but your interpretation changes as you alter the lens. Sometimes we interpret situations without enough information. Other times, we have all the evidence, but we need to decide what point of view we want.

Reframing is not changing the situation or denying reality. It is an intentional choice to look at an event using a different lens or point of view. Reframing becomes easier as we work on our core beliefs (see Chapter 6, "Determining Our Core Beliefs"). The story I shared about Victor Frankl in the last chapter is an excellent example of reframing. He lived in the worst conditions possible, but he found meaning in his circumstances. He chose to interpret his experiences in the most favorable light he could.

How do we reframe anxiety-provoking circumstances? Let's say I have a terrible headache. I interpret the headache as *I have a brain tumor*. I tend to catastrophize. Therefore, I want to be intentional with how I chose to view my headache. The reality is, "I have a headache," but just because I believe I have a brain tumor doesn't mean I actually have a brain tumor. Remember, we don't want to believe every thought we think. Anxious thoughts are almost always inaccurate. I decide my new explanation for my headache is that I'm dehydrated. I drink some water, maybe take an aspirin, and move on. Sometimes it helps to get a non-anxious loved one involved. I can count on my husband to give me non-anxious interpretations.

If you decide to consult a friend, be sure not to consult an anxious friend. I did this with a girlfriend who also struggles with anxiety. Years ago, I told her how nervous I was that Patrick was taking my boys surfing on some big waves. I explained to her my fear of them being eaten by sharks. Her response was, "Sharks! I would be afraid they would hit their heads and drown." My anxiety spiked. When asking for help with these practices, choose wisely.

We can also reframe a situation by looking through the eyes of Christ. When we try to have an eternal perspective, everything changes.

James 1:2 tells us to "consider it pure joy, my brothers [and sisters], whenever you face trials of many kinds." What? How do we find joy in suffering? To do this, we must look through an eternal lens. Having an eternal perspective can be difficult when we are in pain. To have this kind of perspective, we need to remember that the most essential part of us is our soul. Our holiness is much more important than our happiness. I believe God will allow suffering if it means our souls are more prepared for eternity. This doesn't mean that God creates all suffering for this purpose. However, because he uses all things for good (Romans 8:28), he will even use for good the pain caused by evil.

In the book of Genesis, we read about a man named Joseph. Joseph went through great suffering, partially due to his brothers selling him into slavery. God used Joseph in mighty ways over many years. Near the end of this story, Joseph sees his brothers, and instead of condemning them, he says to them, "What you meant for evil against me, God used for good" (Genesis 50:20 author paraphrase).

Most of us can think of a challenging time in our lives when we couldn't understand why an event was happening. However, over time we saw how God used a painful event to develop something within us that needed refining. Or maybe we understood that the trial protected or prepared us. We can reframe our circumstances by reminding ourselves of God's faithfulness. Do you have any past or present circumstances you need to reframe?

Thought Stopping

Thought stopping can effectively reduce anxiety as long as you use additional techniques such as mindfulness, meditation, and assessing positive memories. With thought stopping, you first have to be aware that you are having an anxious thought. After you have the awareness, you say to yourself, *Stop*. Saying *stop* out loud is more powerful but not necessary (especially if you are in public). You then quickly focus on something else. I prefer to say to myself, *Stop*, and then think upon Scripture verses that I have preplanned to ponder. By doing this, you not only stop the anxious thought, but you also fill your mind with God's Word and keep any spiritual warfare at bay.

I encourage you to plan what you will use to replace your anxious thoughts when you are using this exercise. You can think about anything that distracts you from your anxious thought. The key to this technique is to activate your prefrontal cortex. You can do a math problem, think of a yoga pose you are working on, or bring forth a positive memory. Using brain teasers (see the "Brain Teasers" on the next page) with thought stopping works great. We should only use distraction to reduce anxiety when we are in a situation where we cannot deal with our anxiety at that moment, such as being in a meeting or a class. If we used distraction all the time, we would never get to the root of the problem.

Brain Teasers

Brain teasers work great with thought stopping. Remember, when we are experiencing significant anxiety, our amygdala has hijacked our thinking brain. Therefore, we want to trigger our prefrontal cortex (PFC) to calm the amygdala and get us thinking clearly. One way to do this is with a technique called brain teasers. Brain teasers are easy to do, especially if you catch the highjack early. The less the PFC is functioning, the harder it is to activate the thinking brain. Brain teasers are a way to trigger the PFC by asking it questions. Write three questions on a notecard. The sky is the limit as to what you can ask yourself. The questions need to be challenging but not impossible to answer. For instance, you can write: *Name ten presidents, Complete a complex math problem, and Name your first- through sixth-grade teachers.* After the questions become easy, make a new one. You can also ask someone to make the notecards for you so the questions will be unknown until you use them. Carry the notecard in your purse or pocket.

Brain teasers work great with kids. I used the brain teaser technique with John when he saw Santa. As the parent or friend, you don't need a notecard. Just start asking questions. The key is to help them engage their thinking brain. Remember to avoid *why* questions, because those can trigger more emotion. The questions you choose will depend on the age of the child. For a young child, you can ask them to count numbers or recite the alphabet. You can ask an older child what they had for a snack yesterday or ask an off-the-wall question to get their attention. You can also ask how many jumping jacks your child can do in one minute, have them climb a tree, or go for a run. You can help your child develop their own notecards. This does not always work, especially with older kids. I have heard that some parents have received some choice words when they tried this with their teenagers. Be creative. Find what works with your child.

Worry Time

Worry time is another excellent exercise to implement for those who wake in the night with anxious thoughts, or your work is being affected by the number of anxious thoughts you have. For worry time, you put on your schedule ten to thirty minutes (depending on the amount of worry you have) every day when all you do is worry. Be sure not to schedule your worry time just before you go to bed. Worrying right before bed can make falling asleep more challenging.

I know this may sound crazy, but it can be very effective for some. You must be faithful to take the time to worry during your scheduled worry time if you want this to work. During your worry time, write all the things that worry you. Writing your worries is much more powerful than thinking or even talking about them. Let it out. Then when you have anxious thoughts during the day, are trying to fall asleep, or wake up in the middle of the night, you tell yourself, *I can worry about that during my worry time, not now.* Promise yourself that you will take care of the worrying during your next scheduled worry time. Many people are surprised by how well this works at reducing anxiety. As they practice this behavior, they find that they don't need as much worry time on their schedule. The key is to worry well, but only once.

Sometimes we worry because there is a problem to address or solve. For instance, you have heard your company is laying off people next month. You haven't been there long and are concerned that you will be laid off. There may be steps you can take to reduce your concerns. For instance, you can sit down with your boss and ask if your job is in jeopardy. You can start looking for another job, just in case. Do your problem solving during your worry time, and then let it go.

Gratitude Journal

Everyone would benefit from keeping a gratitude journal, anxious or not. Gratitude journaling is very effective in reducing anxiety and depression. Any type of journaling is good for you. It is a great way to process life experiences. For a gratitude journal, write at least one thing you are thankful for every day. Most people end up writing more than one. Studies have found gratitude is strongly and consistently associated with greater happiness. Gratitude helps people feel more positive emotions, relish good experiences, improve their health, deal with adversity, and build strong relationships.[37] By instilling gratitude into our brains, we are rewiring and renewing our minds.

God's Word often talks about thankfulness and its benefits. First Thessalonians 5:18 says, "Give thanks in all circumstances." Philippians 4:6 says, "By prayer and petition with thanksgiving, present your requests to God." The Book of Psalms has numerous verses on thanksgiving. My favorite is: "Enter his gates with thanksgiving and his courts with praise; give thanks to him and praise his name" (Psalm 100:4). In her book *Armor of God*, Priscilla Shirer says this about thankful prayer: "When we choose thankful prayer over wallowing in anxiety and worry, we are demonstrating an unwavering trust in God. Prayer shrouded in gratitude expresses a firm faith. Concentrating on him instead of being absorbed by our circumstance tells the Lord that we believe he can override and overcome even the most difficult issues. This kind of faith catches his attention, and he responds by activating his peace within us—a peace that not only *guard* but will *guide* us by helping us discern the direction God is leading us to take in our lives."[38] Gratitude is good for the soul, mind, and body.

Just a side note to journaling: I keep a Scripture journal, a list of verses that have touched my heart. I started the journal during a dark time in my life and have kept adding to it during the hard times and the joyful times. It is something I will always treasure. I reread the verses regularly and am always encouraged. Consider starting one. You will not regret it.

Being thankful goes far beyond keeping a gratitude journal. Fill your heart, your mind, and your life with thankfulness.

Application:

Write down a fear you need to face, and come up with steps of exposure.

_____

_____

_____

Questions:

1. What cognitive-behavioral technique from this chapter would you most likely implement into your life? Why?

_____

_____

_____

2. Which one would you least likely attempt? Why?

_____

_____

_____

CHAPTER 9
WAYS TO REWIRE OUR BRAINS

Do not conform any longer to the pattern of this
world, but be transformed by the renewing of
your mind. Then you will be able to test and
approve what God's will is—his good, pleasing,
and perfect will. — Romans 12:2

Three minutes seems like an eternity. *Please God, let there be two pink lines this time. I can't take another negative test.* My stomach is churning, and I feel a lump in my throat. Four minutes have gone by, and still no second line. My heart aches. Will I ever get pregnant? *Lord, I have been praying for a child for so many years now. It is such a wholesome request, and yet you haven't answered it. Why, can't you hear my cries and see my anguish? I feel so alone on this journey of infertility. I can't seem to tell my family or friends what we are going through. I am afraid my feelings will be minimized, or people will see me as defective.*

For five years, my husband and I went through infertility. It wasn't until year three that we shared what we were going through. At the time, I didn't understand how much sharing my story would be an essential part of my healing. Sharing our stories can rewire our brains.

Much of what we have talked about can help us rewire our brains. Reducing anxiety with relaxation techniques and cognitive-behavioral exercises are all ways we rewire our brains. We rewire our brains by taking every thought captive. By reducing our anxiety, we are pruning the neuropathways that lead to anxiety. By rethinking our childhood and adult experiences, we are rewiring how we think of our past and changing those memory pathways. But we can do more. We can create more positive, healthy experiences—new pathways, new memories, and therefore, new ways of living life.

Sharing Our Stories

As iron sharpens iron, so a friend sharpens a friend. — Proverbs 27:17 (NLT)

One way to rewire our brains is to share our stories, which is a type of exposure or a way of facing our fears. Sharing our stories with others does several beautiful things. First, it connects us to people, one of the most important ways to improve our mental and spiritual health.

For twenty years, I have been in a prayer group with three women. The time with them has changed my life more than any other activity—except for meditating on God's Word and prayer. I could write a book on this subject. Deep, intimate, safe, and loving relationships are one of God's primary tools to heal us. We consider our group a prayer/accountability group. I can share anything with these women and know I will be loved and accepted, no matter what. I also know, if I am in sin, they will call me out. There is much healing in being accepted by people. There is also great power in believers praying together before God. "Where two or three come together in my name, there am I with them" (Mathew 18:20).

In his book *Lifesigns*, Henri Nouwen says this about being vulnerable in relationships: "A fruitful life is, first of all, lived in vulnerability. As long as we remain afraid of one another, we arm ourselves and live defensive lives. No fruits can come forth from such lives. They lead to walls, arms, and to the most sophisticated inventions, such as *Trident* submarines and cruise missiles, but they do not bear fruit. Only when we dare to lay down our protective shields and trust one another enough to confess our shared weakness and needs can we live a fruitful life together."[39]

I know this can be challenging for some. Being vulnerable is scary. No one wants to be judged or ridiculed. Most of us have experienced some kind of betrayal, which can cut deep and leave us guarded and skeptical about being honest with anyone. I get it. However, when we don't allow ourselves to be vulnerable, we won't experience what it's like to be seen or heard. Being known is a cornerstone to our mental well-being. When we don't allow ourselves to be seen and heard, we can feel a deep loneliness. We cannot be known if we do not share who we are. And sharing who we are can help others share in return. When we experience being seen and heard by others, we build more confidence to share again. Being authentic deepens relationships and our sense of being a part of something bigger.

Social media can make this difficult. When we look at social media, we see people with what appears to be perfect lives. Everyone looks their best. Everyone is happy. No one seems to have any problems—except for you—except for me. I was talking with a friend of a friend. She said she wished she had our mutual friend's life. Little did she know, our mutual friend was suffering intensely. No one's life is perfect. We all have struggles. We benefit by sharing those struggles with safe people. If you don't have anyone safe, I encourage you to get involved in a group Bible study, a sport you enjoy, a club, or a therapeutic group. Let yourself be known.

Another benefit of sharing our stories is learning from one another. Have you ever heard someone share their pain, felt empathy for them, and then felt connected to them? You were reminded that you are not alone in your own pain. Recently in my Bible study, we went around the room and shared a time when God provided for us during a challenging time. The stories were amazing. Sarah shared that she prayed for years that God would heal her marriage. There had been times when she was ready to give up and leave her husband, but she stuck it out and continued to pray and be prayed for. Sarah now has a vibrant relationship with her husband. It's not perfect, but it's good, and she is happy. She and her husband were laughing hysterically about something in the kitchen, and she thought, *Wow, I would have missed this if I had given up on my marriage.* Through her story, we were all mindful of God's faithfulness.

Sharing our stories also helps us process our experiences, and each time we process our experiences, we heal a little more. We gain a little more insight into ourselves and our situations. Have you ever noticed when you have gone through a stressful event—like a car accident, a difficult person on the street, or a big event on the news—you want to call people and talk about it? You want to tell everyone about the experience. We do this with exciting stories as well. We want to tell everyone about the fun party we went to or the fantastic thing our child did for the first time. Why do we do this? Because every time we tell our story, we release some of the emotion connected to the experience, whether positive or negative. Can you hear yourself saying, *You would not believe what happened today.* We feel a little less scared and a little less sad each time we tell a scary or tragic story. With happy stories, we love to relive those euphoric emotions. When we avoid telling others about our more intense experiences and keep our feelings bottled up, our hearts become heavier. I love what Ann Voskamp says in her book *The Broken Way*: "The wounds that never heal are always the ones mourned alone."[40] We need one another.

If we share our stories with the right people, we can rewire how we feel about our experiences. When we share a challenging experience with someone who can provide us with compassion and empathy, that memory changes a little. When we do this repeatedly and receive understanding and empathy, we start to connect the difficult experience with compassion and empathy. Having those two experiences happening together changes the neuropathway of that experience. Now, when we think of that painful memory, we connect it to someone having compassion for us. The pain of the memory lessens, and hopefully, we can experience some peace and joy, because we are reminded that we are loved and cared for, despite our pain. Sharing our story doesn't change what happened, but it changes our reaction to what happened. That gives us such hope.

Extending compassion changes not only the person receiving but also the person giving.

I recall sharing my story of growing up with an alcoholic father. My dear friend Camden showed me compassion. She told me I was a survivor. I had never heard that before, nor had I thought of myself as being a survivor. Those words empowered me. Whenever I shared my story after that, I connected the experience with being a survivor and felt added strength.

Share your story with others. Of course, try to choose safe people. You don't want to share with someone you believe will say, "So what? You should hear what I went through." Or, "Don't be such a baby. Lots of people go through that." Those types of people will not help rewire your brain. Another type of person to avoid is the one who says, "You just need to forgive that person and move on." They may mean well, but they are probably not going to help you heal. I love what Drs. John Townsend and Henry Cloud say in their book *Safe People*: "Safe people are individuals who draw us closer to being the people God intended us to be. Though not perfect, they are 'good enough' in their character that the net effect of their presence in our lives is positive. They are accepting, honest, and present, and they help us bear good fruit in our lives."[41] Noticed that they said *safe people* are not perfect, but they are *good enough*. By the way, telling your story has other benefits in addition to what I have already mentioned, so next time you go to a funeral, ask people to share their stories and see what happens.

Some of you may not believe you have someone you can trust to share your story with. I know what that feels like. There was a time when I was so lonely. I had people in my life, but I didn't *feel* I had a single person I could trust enough to share my heart. I asked God to bring me a friend. With my therapist's help and God's grace, I knew I

94

needed to put out more effort to meet like-minded women. If you had told me then how many wonderful women I would have in my life today, I would have laughed. God gave me more than I asked or imagined, and he will do the same for you. Remember to do your part as God guides you. For those in that lonely place, waiting to establish new friendships, share your story by writing it like an autobiography. After you write your experiences, read them from the perspective of a dear friend. Respond to your story as a trusted friend would. Empathize with the painful parts of your narrative and celebrate the happy parts. Writing our experiences also helps us consolidate our memories and gives us the clarity we may not get by just talking about them.

My friend Camden, who said I was a survivor, also said I needed more compassion for myself. When I shared my story with her, I said several times, "It was no big deal." She told me it was a big deal, and I needed to listen to my story as if a child were telling it—and I was the listener. She asked how I would respond to a little girl who told me the same story I had just told her. I was blown away. Of course, I would not have said it was no big deal. I would have held that little girl in my arms and comforted her. Do the same for yourself. Love that child you once were. Give yourself compassion and empathy and see how it changes how you view your story. Compassion is one of the greatest gifts we can give ourselves and others.

Create Positive Experiences

Create Beautiful Moments.
— Minna So

Another rewiring technique is creating experiences that bring you the trait you want to live out. Creating experiences can apply to any character trait or fruit of the Spirit you desire to implement. Because this book is about reducing anxiety, we will talk about increasing our peace, an antonym of worry.

I hope most of you have experienced peace in your life so you have a mental model of what peace looks and feels like. If you don't have that mental model, find someone who you can emulate. Join a life group or go to a local church and find a mentoring program. Put people in your life who have experienced peace. Meditate on Bible verses that talk about peace. "The fruit of the Spirit is love, joy, peace, patience, kindness, goodness, faithfulness, gentleness, and self-control" (Galatians 5:22). God tells us in Philippians 4:7 that "we get the peace of God that transcends all understanding by being anxious for nothing and bringing everything in prayer to God with thanksgiving" (author paraphrase). It sounds like, as we lessen our anxiety by implementing effective techniques—praying, and giving thanks—we will have the peace that surpasses all understanding.

We become more peace-filled when we repeatedly install experiences of peace. What experiences can we create that will give us a sense of peace? What brings you peace? I experience peace by being in the Word of God, praying in the Spirit, meditating on who God is and who I am in Christ. I can also experience peace when I expose myself to God's creation. Going to the beach and being mindful of my surroundings brings me peace. All these things reduce my anxiety and at the same time bring me more peace. I can also ask myself, *What brings me anxiety?* I experience more fear when I'm tired or too busy. When watching the news, I endure a lot more anxiety. I especially have more fear when I let my thoughts run wild. Therefore, I know to take care of my needs, to avoid too much news, and to be intentional about captivating my thoughts. Every day, try to create experiences that bring you peace.

You can apply this to compassion, gratefulness, or any trait you want to develop. You can also implement this exercise as you work toward changing a core belief. For instance, if the value of a core belief is based on performance, you can counteract this false belief by creating experiences where you are cared for without performing.

Join a Bible study or a prayer group, or be a part of a mission trip where you can develop relationships based on love and mutual respect that doesn't depend on what you can offer someone. Commit time to an animal shelter, because animals are great for their unconditional love. Volunteer at a facility for the disabled or elderly. Spend time with people who desire to connect with you because of who you are not for what you do for them.

If one of your issues is related to feeling inadequate, create experiences where you can feel self-confident. Create new skills that will help you feel good about yourself. Discover what your gifts are and use them to bless others. Fill your life with experiences that bring you fulfillment, joy, and peace—experiences that help you develop patience or require you to do acts of kindness. Even if you don't want to be kind, be kind anyway. Have you ever heard the motto, "Fake it until you make it?" When we practice something over and over, it becomes a habit. If you have a false belief about yourself, such as *I am stupid*, challenge that belief by acknowledging all the proof you have that this view of yourself is not accurate (I can read, I can do math problems, I can get from one place to another). Then write on sticky notes, *I am smart,* or *I am lovable*. Post them everywhere. Every time you see the note, read it out loud. Over time, you will begin to believe you are smart or lovable. Speak truth into yourself. These traits will start to develop and become part of who you are.

Creating positive experiences does not just help us develop godly traits, but they also help us replace harmful material inside our minds. For example, if you have experienced loneliness, begin to create events that fill your life with connection and fellowship. The memories of feeling lonely will dissipate as the fresh memories of connection increase and fill your heart. I am not saying that positive events in your life will eradicate all previous painful memories. I am saying these new experiences can give you some healing and keep your mind focused on the great things happening in your life.

We must speak truth into our lives and the lives of others. The Bible tells us to: Stand firm then, with the belt of truth buckled around your waist (Ephesians 6:14). Truth is an essential part of the armor of God. Remember, never elevate feelings above truth. The truth is, you are loved (Romans 8:38–39), you are a child of God (John 1:12), you are Jesus' friend (John 15:15), you are set free (Galatians 5:1), you are God's workmanship (Ephesians 2:10), you are chosen, holy, and blameless before God (Ephesians 1:4). He is faithful (1 Thessalonians 5:24), he will never leave you (Deuteronomy 31:6), his thoughts of you outnumber the sand of the sea (Psalm 139:17–18), and on and on it goes. Speak God's truth over yourself and to those around you.

Application:

Write one of your life stories and share it with someone.

_____

_____

_____

Questions:

1. What thoughts and feelings come up when you think about sharing your story with someone?

_____

_____

_____

2. What are three positive experiences you would like to create in your life over the next month?

_____

_____

_____

SECTION III
RELAXATION TECHNIQUES: THE BEGINNING
OF LOWERING ANXIETY

*When I understand that everything happening
to me is to make me more Christlike, it resolves
a great deal of anxiety. — A.W. Tozer*

I want to talk about exercises we can implement that will lower the intensity of our fear and the physical responses of anxiety (increase in heart rate and breathing, sweaty palms, butterflies in our stomach). As I mentioned in the "Introduction," I placed the cognitive techniques before the relaxation exercises, because I found that most people want to get to the book's substance first. I consider the cognitive techniques as the meat and the relaxation exercises as the tenderizer for the meat. We must learn to relax to use cognitive techniques more effectively. For many people, practicing the cognitive exercises can create anxiety. Examining our thought life to take our anxious thoughts captive requires us to think about the events that produce anxiety. Therefore, learning to relax will allow us to reduce our anxiety enough to implement the cognitive techniques. Keep in mind, the amygdala needs to experience some anxiety during exposure (facing our anxiety) in order for it to know that the triggering event is not dangerous.

All the disciplines we discuss in this section have been clinically proven to help reduce anxiety.

CHAPTER 10
MEDITATING ON GOD'S WORD

We live, in fact, in a world starved for solitude,
silence, and private: And therefore starved for
meditation and true friendship. — C.S. Lewis

Elizabeth is sitting in her car, hiding. Her car is the only place she can get away from all the noise in her house full of children. She has her Bible and is reading these words: "Do not let your hearts be troubled. Trust in God; trust also in me. In my Father's house are many rooms; if it were not so, I would have told you. I am going there to prepare a place for you. And if I go and prepare a place for you, I will come back and take you to be with me that you also may be where I am. You know the way to the place where I am going" (John 14:1). The words comfort Elizabeth's soul. She meditates on each word to take them in and allow them to change her heart and mind. She knows she can trust God, but it's hard sometimes. She accepts Christ's words that he is preparing a place for her, and she will spend eternity with him. Her heart is troubled because she has taken her eyes off Jesus. This time in the Word has put her thoughts back on him. The Holy Spirit's presence in the car fills Elizabeth with peace. After about fifteen minutes, she is rejuvenated and ready to go back into the chaos.

My favorite relaxation exercise is meditation. Merriam-Webster defines the word meditation as, "The act or process of spending time in quiet thought."[42] Meditation is not passive. It is to think upon something deeply, to rehearse and internalize the information so it becomes part of who you are. Internalizing God's Word is how we renew our minds. Joshua 1:8 says, "Meditate on [the Word] day and night." In verse nine, we are told to *not be terrified.* Isn't it interesting how God puts meditating on his Word alongside not being afraid? Other verses talk about meditating on God's Word:

- I meditate on your precepts and consider your ways. — Psalm 119:15
- Let me understand the teaching of your precepts; then I will meditate on your wonders. — Psalm 119:27
- My eyes stay open through the watches of the night, that I may meditate on your promises. — Psalm 119:148
- Within your temple, O God, we meditate on your unfailing love. — Psalm 48:9

Some Christians might be skeptical about meditation. We sometimes think of the Eastern meditations, which do not come from a biblical perspective. Meditation based on biblical principles is quite different from Eastern meditations that attempt to *empty* the mind. Christian meditation attempts to *fill* the mind. We want to fill our minds with God's Word. We want to be still and listen for the voice of God. Meditating on Scripture focuses on internalizing and personalizing the Word of God. Richard Foster in his book *Celebration of Discipline* describes meditation beautifully. He says, "Inward fellowship of this kind transforms the inner personality. We cannot burn the eternal flame of the inner sanctuary and remain the same, for the Divine Fire will consume everything impure. Our ever-present Teacher will always be leading us into 'righteousness and peace and joy in the Holy Spirit' (Romans 14:17)." Foster also writes: "The meditation of Scripture centers on internalizing and personalizing the passage. The written Word becomes a living word addressed to you."[43] God wants to speak to us and encourage us through his Word.

We have talked about the wiring and rewiring of the brain. We must take captive our anxious thoughts to lessen the strength of our *anxious* pathways in our brains. We must also replace and create new neuropathways that are healthy and bring peace. Meditation is an exercise that does both. Meditating on God's Word creates healthy new circuits in our brain. James 1:21 tells us that "the Word of God planted in us can save our souls" (author paraphrase).

There is no one right way to meditate on God's Word. Some theologians recommend picking a verse and meditating on it daily for a week. Write your thoughts and prayers as you meditate. Then you can reread what you have learned and heard from God. Here is an example of meditating on a specific Scripture for one week.

- Day 1: Take one or two verses and read them over and over for two minutes.
- Day 2: Ask yourself, *What is God saying in these verses?*
- Day 3: Ask yourself, *What do these verses say about who God is?*
- Day 4: Ask yourself, *What is God saying to me in these verses?*
- Day 5: Ask yourself, *How does God want me to respond to these verses?*
- Days 6 and 7: Go over the first five days of notes and spend time being still and listening for God's voice. Take time to worship your Father for who he is.

Meditate on these things, and allow God to speak to your heart. Don't be surprised when you become distracted. As soon as you notice your distraction, go back to reading the verse. As you can focus longer, add more time to your meditation practice. Then add more verses. Be still, and listen for the Holy Spirit to minister to you. "Be still and know that I am God" (Psalm 46:10).

Using the bullet points above, here's an example of what it might look like to meditate on God's Word using verses related to reducing anxiety.

- Day 1: I ask God to speak to my heart and mind through my time in the Word. Then I read Philippians 4:6–7. "Do not be anxious about anything, but in every situation, by prayer and petition, with thanksgiving, present your requests to God. And the peace of God, which transcends all understanding, will guard your hearts and your minds in Christ Jesus." Slowly I read the verses several times, then finish my meditation with praise, confession, thanksgiving, and petitions.

- Day 2: I ask God to teach and guide me through my meditation. I reread the verses and ask, "What is God saying in these verses?" God is saying, *Do not worry about any situation. Instead pray and bring everything to him, with thanksgiving.* Then, he will give a peace that is beyond understanding. Through Christ, the Father will guard our hearts and minds. I finish my meditation with praise and thanksgiving.

- Day 3: I ask God to speak to me as I contemplate his Word. I reread the verses, and ask myself, *What do these verses say about who God is?* As I ponder the words, I see that God is loving. He is a Father who wants to hear from his children. His words tell me he is faithful, and he wants what is best for his children. These verses also tell me that God is peace. He desires to give a peace that is beyond understanding. I finish my time with praise of who God is.

- Day 4: I begin with asking God to work in my heart and mind, to change me to be more like him. I read Philppians 4:6–7 and ask myself, *How do these verses speak to me?* I sense God is saying that instead of worrying about my situation, he wants me to lay my fears at his feet, pray about them, ask him for his peace and wisdom, and give thanks for who he is and all he has done and will do. His Words also say that he loves me. He wants what is best for me. He is in control. I end my meditation with thanking God for my relationship with him. I lay my burdens and anxieties at his feet. I thank him for the peace he provides. I confess my sins, and praise him for who he is.

- Day 5: I go before God and ask him to open my heart and mind to his Word. I read the verses, and ask myself, *How does God want me to respond to these verses?* As I meditate on the verses throughout the week and talk with Jesus about my anxiety, my fears lessen. When I sense anxiety about this issue, I go straight to the Lord. Because laying the burden at his feet helps relieve some of my anxiety, I want to do this as soon as I experience worry. The longer I allow myself to worry, the stronger the fear becomes. Then I pray, remembering who God is and what he has done. He is so worthy of my trust. I give him thanks for his peace, the peace that passes all understanding.

- Days 6 and 7: I reread the verses and the journaling I did the first five days. I spend time in quiet meditation. Then I worship my heavenly Father.

Your response to the questions for each day will be different from mine. How God wants you to respond to the verse may differ from how he wants me to respond. Each person needs to listen for his still small voice and hear what he wants to say directly to you. You can add verses, or you can do all the steps in one day. Find what works for you. The goal is to spend time in God's Word and enjoy his presence.

I strongly encourage you not to rush through your meditation of Scripture. The goal is not to get through the verses but to get the verses through you. It's how we renew our hearts and minds.

Application:

Pick a Bible verse to meditate on for a week. You can use the technique from this chapter or use another meditation exercise you are familiar with. Write your thoughts and prayers each day.

_____

_____

_____

_____

_____

_____

_____

_____

Questions:

1. What are your thoughts about meditating on God's Word?

_____

_____

_____

2. How did meditating on the verse you chose impact you? Was it beneficial? If so, in what way? If not, try another verse or meditate on a verse with someone and discuss your experience.

_____

_____

_____

CHAPTER 11
MINDFULNESS

Some people spend so much time worrying about what might happen that they never enjoy what is happening. Take one day at a time. Today, after all, is the tomorrow you worried about yesterday. — Billy Graham

Imagine . . .

A ferocious tiger is pursuing you. You run as fast as you can but come to the edge of a cliff. Glancing back, you see the tiger about to pounce. Fortunately, you notice a rope hanging over the edge of the cliff. You grab it and scramble down, out of reach of the tiger. A close escape! But now, you look down. Five hundred feet below, you see jagged rocks. You look up. The tiger is crouched and waiting . . . and you see two hungry mice, gnawing on the rope. What to do? Nearby, on the face of the cliff, you notice a strawberry. Carefully, you reach out, pluck it, and eat it whole. "Yum!" you say. "That's the most delicious strawberry I ever tasted in my whole life."

This is an ancient story retold by Brennan Manning. After he tells this story, he asks readers an intriguing question: "What does this story tell us? Seize the gift of this moment! If you are preoccupied with the rocks below or the tiger above—with your past or your future—you will miss the strawberry that God wants to give you in the present moment."[44] This is mindfulness. It is being in the present where life is happening.

Mindfulness is another excellent exercise to reduce anxiety and depression. It involves bringing your attention to what is happening in the moment without drifting to concerns about the past or the future. Since depression comes from thinking of the past and anxiety comes from thinking of the future, staying in the present is the best place, because it is where life happens.

Most of our minds drift quite easily. When this happens, bring your attention back to the present without judging yourself for being distracted. As you practice mindfulness, you may have to redirect your thoughts to the present dozens of times. As you become more skilled, your mind will drift less and less. "Mindfulness allows us to interrupt automatic, reflective fight, flight, or freeze reactions—reactions that can lead to anxiety, fear, foreboding, and worry. By bringing mindfulness to our actual experience in the moment, we can increase the likelihood of exerting more conscious control over our behaviors and attitudes."[45]

There are different views on mindfulness as well as several styles of mindful exercises. Because mindfulness has Eastern religious origins, we need to understand the difference between an Eastern or Buddhist point of view and a Christian point of view. Buddhists believe the awareness gained through mindful meditation is a power that helps them reach enlightenment. To a Buddhist, enlightenment is to find the truth about life and reach Nirvana, which breaks the cycle of death and rebirth or reincarnation. When I speak of mindfulness or meditation, I am not referring to Eastern thought. Christian mindfulness is being in the moment and focusing on what experiences God has put in front of you right here, right now. Isaiah 43:18 says, "Forget the former things; do not dwell on the past." Matthew 6:34 says, "Do not worry about tomorrow, for tomorrow will worry about itself." Therefore we don't need to think about the past or worry about the future. Live in today. The more we stay in the present, the more we experience life.

108

You can be in the present moment by focusing on whatever you are doing. The key is to use your five senses as much as possible. If you are doing the dishes, you can stay in the moment by focusing on the water temperature and the soap's feel on your hands. Listen to the clanking of the dishes and the running of the water. Notice the smell of the dish soap you are using. Use as many of your senses as possible.

Another example is being mindful while taking a walk on the beach. Feel the sand between your toes. Notice the smells of the ocean. Listen to the crashing of the waves. Enjoy the beauty of God's creation.

I teach a four-week course on anxiety. At the end of every course, I ask participants what their favorite exercise was. The majority of the attendees say the mindfulness practice. It may be because I use chocolate, but I think it's because mindfulness is such a peaceful experience. Let's be mindful together. Get yourself a piece of chocolate or anything that sounds delightful to you. I always provide carrot sticks for those who don't eat chocolate. Be aware, it is common to be distracted. Thoughts will pop into your head that don't belong there while trying to be mindful. It's okay. When you catch yourself drifting, bring yourself back to your exercise. Focus on your five senses. Let's walk through this step-by-step. There will be actions that I mention that may not fit your experience, because you are using something other than chocolate. Just ignore those and allow yourself to follow along as much as possible.

Let's begin:

- First, take two slow, deep breaths.
- Through your nose, take a deep breath in.
- Hold it for a second.
- Then breathe out through your mouth.
- Repeat.
- Take your chocolate out of its wrapper.
- *Listen* to the noise the foil makes as you open the candy.

- *Look* at the piece of chocolate in your hand.
- *Notice* the dark brown color and the name of the candy etched into the chocolate.
- Be aware of how the candy *feels* on your fingers. Is it beginning to melt? Does it *feel* smooth, or does it have nuts that give the candy a rougher *texture?*
- Now, *smell* the candy. What does it *smell* like? What does the *smell* remind you of? Do you notice any other *smells* besides the cocoa? Maybe caramel, sea salt, almonds, or peanut butter.
- Take a moment to enjoy the *fragrance* the candy gives off.
- Take a small bite of the candy.
- How does it *taste*? Is the cocoa *flavor* the dominant *taste,* or is it something else? Is there any hint of sea salt, caramel, or mint? I hope it *tastes* incredible.
- As you chew the chocolate, *feel* the chocolate on your tongue.
- Swirl it around your mouth. Is it smooth? Is it slippery? Is there any chocolate on your lips or fingers?
- When you chew, is there any *noise* the candy makes in your mouth? Can you *smell* the chocolate while you are chewing?
- Go ahead and swallow the chocolate.
- *Feel* it go down your throat. Did it go down smoothly?
- Swallow again and enjoy the *flavors* as the chocolate goes down.
- Put the rest of the chocolate in your mouth.
- Again, notice the *flavors*, the *smell.*
- Be aware of how it *feels* in your mouth.
- *Look* at your fingers and *see* if there is any chocolate stuck to them. If so, lick them clean.
- Enjoy this moment in the present.

How was that? I think I need to stop typing and get a piece of chocolate. Now, I don't recommend always going to chocolate to practice being mindful. We want to be mindful throughout each day. Be intentional about being present no matter what you are doing.

Time and time again, research shows mindfulness is an excellent practice for our mental health. Studies show mindfulness benefits us, not only mentally but also physically, emotionally, and spiritually. Studies show that mindful meditation can help ease psychological stresses like anxiety, depression, and pain.[46]

Dr. Elizabeth Hoge, an assistant professor of psychiatry at Harvard Medical School, says, "Mindful meditation makes perfect sense for treating anxiety. People with anxiety have a problem dealing with distracting thoughts that have too much power. They can't distinguish between a problem-solving thought and a nagging worry that has no benefit." She says, "If you have unproductive worries, you can train yourself to experience those thoughts completely differently. Mindfulness teaches you to recognize, 'Oh, there's that thought again, I've been here before.' But it's just that, a thought, and not a part of my core self."[47] Something as simple as staying present in the moment and not judging yourself when you get distracted can significantly impact your thought processes and anxiety feelings. One study found that people who had participated in an eight-week mindful-meditation program continued to show a decrease in anxiety three years later.[48] The positive effects of the mindfulness practice to reduce anxiety was *still experienced three years later*. That is powerful.

Earlier, we talked about the amygdala, the brain center that regulates anxiety and the fight-flight-freeze response. Research has shown that an eight-week course on mindful meditation practice can shrink the amygdala. As the amygdala shrank, the pre-frontal cortex (the part of the brain responsible for decision making) became thicker. The amount of change correlated to the number of hours in mindful meditation practice.[49] What this means for us is: we can be more thoughtful and less anxious under stress. Yippie!

Being mindful allows us to slow things down and be aware of where our attention is. We become more conscious of the world around us. When we are present, we are more acquainted with our emotions and can make them work *for* us instead of against us. Focused attention also allows us to learn more easily and efficiently.

Being present is where life happens, and the more present we are, the more fulfilling life will be.

It has been said that 40–45 percent of what we do is automatic.[50] This indicates that we don't put thought into what we are doing, because it has become, well, *automatic*. We don't have to think how to get home from work. We drive home and let our minds wander. How much of life do we miss because we are not engaged in the moment? Life is lived in the moment, and when we are not mindful, we miss out.

When my sister and I hike, we take at least one moment to stop and be mindful of our surroundings. We take in our view of the ocean, the puffy clouds in the sky, or the blooming flowers. We try to get an imprint of what we are taking in. The other day, our trail was damp. We noticed thousands of spider webs in the brush, all covered in dew, so they were easy to spot. Everywhere we looked, perfectly made webs were hanging between branches. It was a fantastic sight. We were so grateful for the opportunity to notice not just the beauty but also how amazing God's creation is. Our five senses are such a wonderful gift from God. Use them to help you be present.

Application:

Take five or ten minutes to be mindful.

Questions:

1. What activity were you mindful of? What was the experience like for you?

2. Would you like mindfulness to be part of your daily life? Why or why not?

_____

_____

_____

CHAPTER 12
OTHER RELAXATION EXERCISES

Worry does not empty tomorrow of its sorrows.
It empties today of its strength.
— Corrie Ten Boom

Honk, honk! What are you waiting for? Don't you see the light is green?

Move over. Why did you get in my lane? I'm in a hurry, lady! I'm going to be late for my Bible study. I wish people would pay attention. Look at that kid on his phone. No wonder he is driving so slow. I hate being late. It stresses me out. If I am late, I am not setting a good example to the other ladies. Oh, shoot! Michelle is waving at me. I hope she didn't see me, her Bible study leader, rip around that SUV. Here I go again, driving like a maniac to be on time. I need to chill out.

I take some deep breaths and relax my shoulders. I turn on some praise music to calm my spirit. *Just breathe. I will get there when I get there.*

Some other helpful exercises to reduce anxiety and increase relaxation are: deep breathing, progressive muscle relaxation, and accessing positive memories. Some of you might be thinking, *How am I supposed to do all of these things?* You might be feeling a great deal of anxiety, just thinking about it. I encourage you: most of these ideas take very little time. You can practice deep breathing while you are

114

driving or sitting at your computer. Accessing positive memories doesn't take any time either. I will talk about several other helpful techniques in this book, but you do not have to do all of them to reduce anxiety. Try several of them to determine which ones benefit you the most.

Deep Breathing

Often, when we feel anxious, we breathe more quickly, and our breaths become shallow. Rapid, shallow breathing is a typical symptom when we are in the fight-flight-freeze response. By taking control of our breathing, we tell our brains, specifically our amygdala, that we are okay and don't need to be in the stress response.

Deep breathing is one of the most common types of mindfulness techniques. Research shows breath control helps quiet unnecessary stress responses.[51] Deep breathing is learning to take proper deep breaths while you focus on the breath itself. There are a few types of deep breathing. The most effective is diaphragmatic breathing or belly breathing. Belly breathing is my go-to anxiety-reducing technique. I use it every day. I focus on deep breaths in line at the grocery store, driving my car, or before I have something challenging to do. Practicing slow, deep breaths calms me immediately.

With rapid, shallow breathing, we don't exhale enough carbon dioxide (CO_2) and don't inhale enough oxygen (O_2), which can cause dizziness and numbness in the hands and face. Anyone who has had a panic attack can relate to what I am saying. This type of breathing can add or intensify physical symptoms of anxiety. Deep breathing helps us relax and focus. It also balances the amount of oxygen and carbon dioxide that our bodies need. Deep breathing is easy to do, and we can implement it anytime and anywhere. Proper deep breathing is done slowly, deeply, and mostly with our belly. Watch a baby or puppy breathe. They breathe primarily with their bellies. The diagram below shows that when we push our bellies out as we breathe in, our lungs expand, allowing more oxygen to enter our lungs.

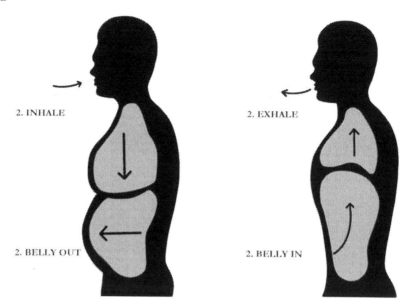

In addition to expanding our lungs, belly breathing stimulates the vagus nerve. The vagus nerve is the longest cranial nerve running from the brain stem to the colon. Two important things happen when we stimulate the vagus nerve. It releases anti-anxiety chemicals into the body, and it activates the parasympathetic nervous system (PNS). If you recall our discussion on brain functioning and anxiety, the PNS is responsible for the relaxation response. Seventy-five percent of all parasympathetic nerve fibers in the body come from the vagus nerve. Therefore, when we stimulate the vagus nerve using belly breathing, we impact the PNS, or relaxation response. Deep breathing, especially belly breathing, is an essential tool in our *Victory over Anxiety* toolbox.

To become skilled in deep breathing, we need to spend time practicing.

Instructions for belly breathing:

- First, lie on your back or sit up straight in a comfortable position. Place one hand on your belly just below your ribs and the other hand on your chest.
- Next, take a deep breath in through your nose and let your belly push your hand out. Your hand on your chest should not move. Hold your breath for two to five seconds.
- Then breathe out through your mouth. Your hand on your belly should move inward. You can facilitate your breathing by gently using this hand to push all the air out.

Take your time with each breath. While doing this exercise, be mindful of your breathing. Listen to the sound your breath makes, and feel the air enter your nostrils and leave your mouth. Be aware of your lungs filling with air.

When I use deep breathing, I often add something I learned from Xochitl Dixon in her book *Waiting for God: Trusting Daily in God's Plan and Pace*. At the end of each devotional, she encourages the reader to "inhale the truth of Scripture, exhale prayers of honesty and belief, and find rest in God's enduring love."[52]

Whenever you need to calm yourself and reduce feelings of anxiety, implement belly breathing. Once you are skilled in belly breathing, you will not need to use your hands, and you can practice it in any position. That's it. If you find you struggle with belly breathing, that's okay. Just focusing on your breathing is helpful. Many of us naturally breathe using our chest. If you find you are more comfortable taking slow, deep breaths with your chest versus your belly, give yourself grace and do that. Part of the benefit of deep breathing is the mindfulness of it. Focusing on your breathing improves your awareness of being in the present. Practicing deep breathing for five minutes, three times a day, will increase your awareness of your breath and create a healthy habit.

Here is a great breathing exercise for young children. Get a fragrant flower and a lit candle. Ask children to take a deep breath in and smell the flower. Then ask them to breathe out slowly and blow out the candle. After just a few practices, you can skip the props and encourage them to take their deep breath by smelling the flower and blowing out the candle. You don't have to use props to teach them this technique. It makes it more fun and gives them a great visual, but you can teach them using imagery as well. Talk with them about how good it feels to take slow, deep breaths. Explain in simple terms that this type of breathing can help them calm down and feel less afraid.

Progressive Muscle Relaxation

Progressive Muscle Relaxation (PMR) is another excellent exercise for reducing anxiety.

Remember, a common physical symptom of anxiety is muscle tension. By relaxing your muscles, you are telling your brain you are okay and not anxious. PMR reduces stress and anxiety, increases concentration, helps provide a better outlook on life, improves mood, enhances well-being, increases energy levels, improves sleep, and strengthens the immune system.[53] PMR also decreases cortisol (stress hormone).

Let's practice. When you first learn this technique, it is best to practice in comfortable clothes and no shoes.

- Lie on your back or sit in a comfortable position. Put your arms next to your sides. Try to completely relax and think of a happy memory or a special Bible verse. You can use a relaxation tape if you need more structure.
- First, take a couple of deep breaths, holding them for three seconds. Then take a deep breath in through your nose, and hold it while you tighten your toes and feet. Tighten them as tight as you can for the count of five (holding your breath as you tighten). I like to count by thousandths (one thousand one, one thousand two, up to five). If five seconds is too long, hold for what is comfortable to you. While counting, notice how

tight your toes and feet feel. If you get a cramp, which happens sometimes, stretch and start over or go to the next muscle group. After five seconds, breathe out through your mouth, and relax those muscles. After you have loosened the muscles in your toes and feet, be mindful of how your muscles feel and notice how relaxed they are.

- After relaxing for about five seconds, take another deep breath, tighten your feet and toe muscles again, and add your calf muscles. Count to five slowly, noticing the tension in those muscle groups. Breathe out and relax for about five seconds, catching how relaxed those muscles feel, and then move on to the next muscle group.

The order after the calf muscles is:

- Thighs
- Buttocks
- Pelvic muscles (which includes sphincter and kegel muscles)
- Abdomen
- Chest and back
- Shoulders, arms, and hands
- Neck and face

For each addition, include all the muscle groups you have already done. By the end, you will be tightening every muscle in your body at once. I recommend tightening the whole body a couple of times to complete the exercise. Then take one last deep breath and smile, knowing you have done something good for yourself. After you practice this technique at home and have the hang of it, use it anytime, anywhere. You no longer need to sit or lie down. It might be a little awkward to lie down at work or in line at the grocery store. You don't have to complete the whole process to feel relaxed. Just notice any tension in your body and start relaxing and letting the pressure go. You may need to tighten the strained muscles even more to exaggerate the stress so you can then experience the relief of releasing the tension. After you have relaxed the tightened muscles, notice how relaxed you feel.

Here is a fun muscle-relaxation technique for children. Teach them about the Tinman and the Scarecrow if they have never seen *The Wizard of Oz*. Then show them what it looks like to be the Tinman and Scarecrow. Have them play along with you, encouraging them to pretend being Tinman by tightening up all their muscles. Every muscle should be stiff like tin. Tell them to notice how their muscles feel when they are tight. Then encourage them to pretend to be Scarecrow and make their muscles completely relaxed, as if they didn't have any muscles at all. They may need to flop to the ground. Ask them how their muscles feel when they are like straw. Have them repeat the process as many times as they want. Complete the exercise by asking them what it was like being the two characters. Teach them how good it is for our minds and bodies to relax our muscles when we feel afraid, angry, or stressed. When you notice the child becoming too emotional, tell them it's time for the Tinman-Scarecrow game, and play along with them.

Accessing Positive Memories

I include Accessing Positive Memories to reduce anxiety because it is easy, enjoyable, and you can do it anytime, anywhere. Make a conscious effort to think of a positive memory, one that brings you joy and puts a smile on your face. When you are feeling anxious, it is best to pull up a peaceful memory. This isn't the time to think about when you jumped out of an airplane or swam with sharks. Even though these types of memories might bring you joy, they will likely produce a physical response not conducive to reducing anxiety. The point of retrieving a positive memory is: it brings joy. There are several benefits. Joy promotes a healthier lifestyle, boosts our immune system, helps fight stress and pain, and supports longevity, to name a few.[54] We experience joy when our bodies release dopamine and serotonin, the neurotransmitters that boost mood. Therefore, we can watch videos of puppies or babies to create joy. Think about activities that make you laugh. Even the act of smiling tells our brains that we are experiencing happiness. Even if the smile is fake, we can trick our brains into thinking we are happy, which causes the brain to release our happy chemicals. The saying, "Fake it till you make it," is really true.

We also want to access positive memories, because our frontal lobe is stimulated, which is responsible for cognitive functioning. We know connecting to our frontal lobe helps stave off anxiety, especially amygdala-based anxiety.

If you find only negative memories surfacing, you can focus more on God's Word and other encouraging and uplifting readings. You can listen to upbeat music or recall scenes from a movie that brought you joy. The point is, we need to think upon "whatever is true, whatever is noble, whatever is right, whatever is pure, whatever is lovely, whatever is admirable—if anything is excellent or praiseworthy—think about such things" (Philippians 4:8).

Application:

Take five slow, deep belly breaths, being mindful of the breath itself.

Questions:

1. What were your physical and mental reactions to deep breathing?

2. Did a joyous memory pop into your head when you read about accessing positive memories? If so, what was it? If not, recall one or think about something that creates happiness in you?

_____

_____

_____

SECTION IV
LIFE STYLE MODIFICATIONS
TO REDUCE ANXIETY

Or do you not know that your body is a temple
of the Holy Spirit within you, whom you have
from God? You are not your own, for you were
bought with a price. So glorify God in your
body. — 1 Corinthians 6:19-20 (ESV)

Physical exercise, good nutrition, and adequate sleep are crucial for a healthy mind. This section will discuss specific benefits of exercise, nutrition, and sleep and how each one can contribute to lowering anxiety.

CHAPTER 13
PHYSICAL EXERCISE

The only exercise I excel at is jumping to
conclusions. — James Nathan Miller

Dear Diary,

For my birthday this year, my husband purchased a week of personal training at the local gym. Although I am still in great shape since being a high school cheerleader forty-three years ago, I decided it would be a good idea to go ahead and give it a try.

I called the club and made my reservations with a personal trainer named Christo. He identified himself as a twenty-six-year-old aerobics instructor and model for athletic clothing and swimwear. He encouraged me to keep a diary to chart my progress.

Monday: I started my day at 6:00 a.m. Tough to get out of bed, but I found it was well worth it when I arrived at the gym to find Christo waiting for me. He is something of a Greek god, with blonde hair, dancing eyes, and a dazzling white smile. He was encouraging as I did my sit-ups, although my gut was already aching from holding it in the whole time he was around. This is going to be a fantastic week.

Tuesday: I drank a whole pot of coffee, but I finally made it out the door. Christo made me lie on my back and push a heavy iron bar into the air with weights on it. My legs were a little wobbly on the treadmill, but I made the full mile. His rewarding smile made it all worthwhile. I feel great. It's a whole new life for me.

Wednesday: The only way I can brush my teeth is by laying the toothbrush on the counter and moving my mouth back and forth over it. I believe I have a hernia in both pectorals. Driving was okay as long as I didn't try to steer or stop. I almost parked on top of a little GEO Storm in the club parking lot. Christo was impatient with me, insisting that my screams bothered other club members. His voice is a little too perky for that early in the morning. When he scolds me, he has this annoying, nasally whine. My chest hurt when I got on the treadmill, so Christo put me on the stair monster. Why would anyone invent a machine to simulate an activity rendered obsolete by elevators? Christo told me it would help me get in shape and enjoy life. He said some other crap too.

Thursday: The loser was waiting for me with his vampire-like teeth exposed as his thin, cruel lips were pulled back in a full snarl. I couldn't help being a half-hour late. It took me that long to tie my shoes. He had me work out with dumbbells. When he wasn't looking, I ran and hid in the restroom. He sent some skinny chick to find me. Then, as punishment, he put me on the rowing machine, which I sank.

Friday: I hate Christo more than any human being has ever hated any other human being in the history of the world. He is a stupid, skinny, anemic, anorexic, little aerobics instructor. If there were a part of my body I could move without unbearable pain, I would beat him with it. He wanted me to work on my triceps. I don't have any triceps. And if you don't want dents in the floor, don't hand me the darn dumbbells or anything that weighs more than a sandwich. The treadmill flung me off, and I landed on a health-and-nutrition teacher. Why couldn't it have been someone softer?

Saturday: Satan left a message on my voicemail in his grating, shrilly voice, wondering why I didn't show up today. Just hearing his voice made me want to smash my phone. I lacked the strength to use the TV remote and ended up catching eleven straight hours of *The Weather Channel.*

Sunday: I'm having the church van pick me up for services today so I can go and thank God that this week is over. I will also pray that next year my husband chooses a gift for me that is fun, like a root canal or a hysterectomy. I still say, if God wanted me to bend over, He would have sprinkled the floor with diamonds.[55]

Physical exercise is vital to our health and to reduce anxiety. Some of the benefits of exercise are: weight loss, strengthening the immune system, and lowering heart disease, cancer, diabetes, and stroke. Exercise can improve memory as well as improve learning. It lowers stress, increases self-confidence, improves sleep, and boosts energy. Regular exercise reduces muscle tension and builds brain resources (it helps create neurons and neuropathways in our brains). Exercise also improves resilience, which is defined as the ability to recover quickly from difficulty. Most importantly, for our discussion, it decreases the activation of the amygdala and improves mood.

Serotonin, dopamine, norepinephrine, as well as endorphins are released during exercise. All these neurotransmitters have a positive impact on mood. Research shows physical activity decreases depression, lowers anxiety, as well as helps control ADHD symptoms. Also, physical exercise can be as effective as cognitive behavioral therapy for anxiety and depression. The effects of exercise start immediately and can last forty-eight hours upon completion. If done regularly, the benefits last a lifetime.

If you struggle to exercise regularly, try to find something you enjoy. If you do not like it, you probably won't do it. If you don't enjoy any activity, pick something you can tolerate. If you begin to develop a habit, it might become something you take pleasure in. The American Heart Association recommends you get your heart rate up (high enough that it is challenging to talk) for thirty minutes, five times a week.[56]

Martial arts, dancing, and yoga are excellent exercises that can improve our physical and mental health. These activity modes require the participant to focus on their body, creating a mindful practice. To develop skills in any martial art, dancing, or yoga, you must be aware of every movement you make and what future actions you need to carry out. There is a great deal of mind work going on as you perform such art forms. Also, these workouts require breath control. Because any martial art is a contact sport, which may trigger the stress response, it may not be a good choice for everyone. However, if you are okay with experiencing some exposure, the confidence and self-awareness you will learn from these modalities might be worth a little discomfort. Each of us needs to examine our personal goals and determine what we are willing to expose ourselves to.

I went with my dad to see his neurologist due to some complications he was having. The doctor told him the two best things he could do for his brain and physical health were to exercise and socialize. My dad's response was, "I don't like doing either of those." The doctor gave him several options, and my dad said no to all of them. The doctor told him if he didn't pick some physical activity, his memory would continue to decline, and his body would continue to deteriorate. The next day, my dad tried to be more active by parking two blocks from an appointment. He had to stop halfway to rest, but he did it. If my dad can walk two blocks and then three blocks and then four, you too can do some activity to improve your mental and physical health.

My dear friend Jodi asked me to join her in training for a half marathon many years ago. I thought, *What a joke.* I can't run half a mile, much less thirteen miles, and I *hate* running. She was an avid runner and had been most of her life. She said to give her three months and promised me I would love to run. After a month, I still hated it. She then took me to get some new running shoes. It worked. A week after getting the *right* shoes, I had my first runner's high. I didn't even want to go for a run unless it was at least five miles. We did the half marathon and several others after that. My point is this: give different exercises a try. You will probably find at least one you enjoy. Also, it helps if you have a workout partner. If I weren't meeting someone to exercise, most days I would sleep in.

Besides all the benefits already mentioned, there is another excellent reason to keep our bodies healthy. Our bodies are a temple with the Spirit of God living in us. Let's keep God's house healthy with regular exercise and healthy nutrition. "Do you not know that your body is a temple of the Holy Spirit, who is in you, whom you have received from God? You are not your own; you were bought at a price. Therefore honor God with your body" (1 Corinthians 6:19–20).

Application:

Do some physical exercise for at least twenty minutes today.

Questions:

1. Do you exercise regularly? If so, what do you do? For how long? With whom? If not, what do you need to do to implement regular exercise?

_____

_____

_____

2. What benefits of exercise are you most interested in, and what are three workouts you would like to try?

_____

_____

_____

CHAPTER 14
NUTRITION AND MENTAL HEALTH

You are what you eat.
— Ludwig Andreas Feuerbach

Good nutrition creates good health in all areas of our lives, including our mental health. You've probably heard the expression: "You are what you eat." The food we eat alters the nutrients in our body, and therefore what we eat affects all aspects of our bodies, including our minds. I won't discuss everything there is to know about nutrition and mental health in this short chapter, but I will give you some great information on what our brains need in order to influence better mental health. There are some strong opinions out there on this topic. I am going to attempt to keep the information reasonably basic and neutral. It is essential to keep in mind that some individuals have food sensitivities to whole grains, dairy, or other foods. We need to know our bodies and determine what, if any, foods negatively affect us. A healthy diet that feeds our brains and helps us control our moods is the same regimen recommended to reduce inflammation, weight loss, a healthy heart, and healthy blood sugar. The Mediterranean diet is high in plant-based foods, lean protein, whole grains, and healthy fats.

Plant-Based Foods

Our diet should consist primarily of vegetables. A wide variety of vegetables in various colors is best. Be sure to include plenty of leafy greens. Vegetables provide fiber as well as essential vitamins and minerals. They can help reduce cholesterol and lower the risk of heart disease and some cancers. They are low in calories and have no cholesterol. Fruits are essential in the Mediterranean diet as well. Fruits have various vitamins and minerals we need. Be mindful of how much fruit you eat due to the natural sugar level in some varieties. Berries are a great choice. They are lower in fructose and have anti-inflammatory properties. Cantaloupe, peaches, melons, citrus fruits like oranges, lemons, limes, and grapefruit are great choices. One last fruit that has nearly no sugar is avocados. Yes, they are fruit, and besides having only one gram of sugar in a whole avocado, they provide healthy fats.

Lean Protein

Lean protein is also crucial to a healthy diet. We should be eating about 15–20 grams of lean protein per meal, especially at breakfast. Protein is the building block for neurotransmitters in the brain that affect and regulate mood and many other things. The neurotransmitters more commonly known for regulating mood are serotonin, dopamine, and epinephrine. Without enough protein, our bodies will not have the resources to produce these neurotransmitters at appropriate levels. Examples of lean protein are white fish (halibut, tilapia, cod, haddock, flounder, orange roughy), skinless white-meat poultry, lean beef (less than ten grams of total fat per serving), eggs, beans, lentils, bison, pork tenderloin, lite tofu, and some low-fat dairy. Although higher in calories than white fish, salmon is an excellent source of protein and omega-3 fat.

Whole Grains

The Mediterranean diet includes whole grains as part of a healthy diet. Whole grains have all the parts of the original kernel—bran, germ, and endosperm. In refined grains, the bran and germ are stripped away, taking most of its health benefits. Whole grains are packed with nutrients such as protein, fiber, B vitamins, antioxidants, and trace minerals. A diet rich in whole grains has been shown to reduce heart disease risk, type 2 diabetes, obesity, and some types of cancers. They also help regulate blood sugar. Whole grains contain lactic acid, which promotes good bacteria in the large intestine. These organisms aid in digestion and nutrition absorption and can help strengthen the immune system. Examples of healthy whole-grain choices are barley, wheat, buckwheat, bulgar, steel-oats, millet, and popcorn.

Healthy Fat

In addition to vegetables, lean protein, and whole grains, we need to include healthy fat in each meal. Healthy fats come from polyunsaturated fats and monounsaturated fats, which boost brain function, strengthen our immune system, and improve mood. You can get these healthy fats from avocados, olive oil, flaxseed, nuts, and certain fish (wild-caught salmon, halibut, mackerel, and krill). A vital component we need as part of our healthy fat intake is omega-3 fatty acids. Even if you regularly eat the above foods, it is common to have a deficiency in omega-3. Therefore, supplementing your diet with fish oil is strongly recommended.

Fish Oil

Research has shown there are many benefits to taking fish oil, both for our body and our brain. Fish oil is the source of the most available essential fatty acids, EPA (eicosapentaenoic acid) and DHA (docosahexaenoic acid). Both EPA and DHA are crucial for cell membrane functioning, which controls what goes in and out of cells, including neurotransmitters in the brain and hormone receptors throughout the whole body. Fish oil also has anti-inflammatory effects and is proven to benefit people with ADHD, bipolar disorder, depression, anxiety, heart disease, and arthritis. High doses of EPA and DHA have shown significant prevention of psychosis in ultra-high risk adolescents.[57] Amazing! Take your fish oil daily. To anyone over 100 pounds, Dr. Anne Procyk recommends 1000 mg daily of EPA and 700 mg of DHA. She believes, if you want to see therapeutic results, the dosage needs to be 2000 mg daily of EPA and 1500 mg daily of DHA. What she means by therapeutic dose is the amount needed to see mental health benefits.[58]

Getting high-quality fish oil is essential, mercury and pesticide-free. The packaging must specify the amount of EPA and DHA. If it gives only the total amount of fish oil and does not break it down, don't buy it. Speak with your physician before taking any supplement.

Vitamin B-Complex

In addition to the importance of vegetables, protein, whole grains, and healthy fat, we should consider the importance of vitamins and minerals for mental health and anxiety. Vitamin B-Complex is a combination of all the B vitamins, necessary for optimal adrenal functioning, which helps control blood sugar and burn protein and fat. B vitamins are crucial for the body's ability to make neurotransmitters. It helps our bodies react to stressors, supports blood pressure regulation, and regulates the hormone cortisol, known as the stress hormone. The right amount of cortisol in our bodies helps us fight stress. However, too much cortisol can create several problems, one of which is higher levels of anxiety. Vitamin B-12 deficiency can cause several issues, including depression and anxiety.

We get vitamin B from whole grains, lentils, beans, milk, cheese, eggs, chicken, red meat, fish, dark green vegetables, beets, avocados, nuts, citrus fruits, bananas, soy products, and yeast. Most people need more B vitamins in their diet. Therefore, most of us would benefit from a vitamin B-Complex supplement. When we are under a significant amount of stress, we need more vitamin B-Complex in our system. It is recommended we get 50–100 mg daily of all these B vitamins; B1, B2, B3, B5, B6, B7, B9, and B12. Look for the label B-50 on the bottle, which means you will get at least 50 mg of all these B vitamins in one pill. Take one or two tablets daily with food.[59] B vitamins give us energy, so take the supplement in the morning.

Magnesium

Most of us are deficient in magnesium, an essential mineral for good mental health. It is a stress anecdote, crucial for the relaxation of nerve and muscle cells and excellent for reducing anxiety. Adults need 300–400 mg per day. Magnesium citrate is the most effective form of magnesium, but it can cause diarrhea for some. If you find your body responds this way to magnesium citrate, use magnesium glycinate, which is still effective and doesn't cause bowel issues. Start with one teaspoon in powder form or a 150–200 mg tablet. Magnesium is a calming agent, so take it before bed.

We get some magnesium in eating leafy greens, nuts, beans and legumes, and whole grains. Due to changes in farming practices, not much magnesium comes from our soil. Therefore adding a magnesium supplement to your diet might be beneficial. Mental health signs of possible magnesium deficiency are anxiety, panic attacks, irritability (I already know I need this mineral), poor sleep, and heightened pain sensitivity. I recommend magnesium to anyone who struggles with anxiety.

Calcium

Like magnesium, calcium is another essential mineral, vital for some neurological and muscular functions. Because calcium is much easier to get in the foods we eat, a calcium deficiency is less common than a magnesium deficiency. Too much calcium causes a magnesium deficiency, so you must take a magnesium supplement if you take in a significant amount of calcium. Generally, these two minerals should be taken in equal amounts, including the amount of calcium you consume.

Vitamin D

Vitamin D, also known as the sunshine vitamin due to its ability to be absorbed by the body through sunlight is crucial for absorbing calcium and phosphorus. Vitamin D helps strengthen muscles, supports the immune system, helps fight inflammation, strengthens oral health, helps prevent diabetes, and participates in regulating mood and warding off depression. Foods that include vitamin D are salmon, shrimp, egg yolks, and fortified foods like milk, yogurt, cereal, and orange juice. Sun exposure without sunscreen is another way to get vitamin D. Be sure to limit time in the sun without sunscreen. The recommended dosage for people under seventy years old is 600 IUs, and 800 IUs for those over seventy. IU means international units, another form of measurement used on vitamin D packaging and other vitamins.

Ashwagandha

One last supplement I want to mention is ashwagandha. It sounds like something you would find in the jungles of Central America. Ashwagandha helps with adrenal functions related to anxiety, helps the body reduce excessive cortisol levels (stress hormone), and helps increase resistance to stress, tension, and irritability. It is an adaptogen herb like Ginseng. The recommended dose is 300-500 mg (1–2 capsules, 1–3 times per day).[60] Licorice is another adaptogen herb that helps with anxiety. However, it is not as effective as ashwagandha. I'm not referring to the candy licorice of course, (although that sounds good right now) but to the supplement.

Here is a brief look at daily nutrition recommendations:

- Variety of vegetables throughout the day
- Lean protein (15–20 grams per meal)

- Whole grains
- Healthy fats
- Omega-3 EPA (1,000–2,000 mg), DHA (700–1500 mg)
- Vitamin B-Complex ("B-50" 50–100 mg)
- Magnesium (300–400 mg)
- Calcium (300–400 mg total, including diet)
- Vitamin D (600 to 800 UIs)
- Ashwagandha (1–2 capsules, 1–3 times per day)

Alcohol

A brief comment on alcohol and anxiety: studies indicate that 20 percent of people suffering from social anxiety disorder also suffer from alcohol dependence.[61] Many people with social anxiety use alcohol to feel more confident in social situations. "Alcohol changes levels of serotonin and other neurotransmitters in the brain, which can worsen anxiety. Some people feel more anxious after the alcohol wears off."[62] Not everyone experiences this, but if you find your anxiety increases after consuming alcohol or notice yourself drinking alcohol to cope in social situations, you may want to consider whether drinking alcohol is the best choice for you.

Caffeine

Caffeine and anxiety—a challenging topic for those of you who love your cup of joe first thing in the morning. I understand your pain. Let's at least get educated on the topic so you can decide if caffeine is the right choice for you. Research shows caffeine can affect a person's level of anxiety. Caffeine can significantly affect those who have panic disorder and social anxiety disorder. I have found that those who struggle with generalized anxiety can be negatively affected by caffeine as well. The physical response to consuming caffeine is similar to the symptoms of anxiety. They can both create nervousness, restlessness, increased heart rate, stomach issues, and sleep disturbance. There are two factors that determine if a person who experiences anxiety regularly should consume caffeine.

First, do you find you experience more anxiety after drinking coffee, tea, or energy drinks? My experience working with anxiety sufferers is that the more anxiety they have, the more crucial it is to avoid caffeine. When I first learned this, I was very disappointed. I loved my daily latte. However, I didn't love my latte more than I hated my anxiety, so I gave it up. As I worked on my anxiety over the years, I have found that I can tolerate a small latte or one cup of coffee and not experience anxiety symptoms. Could there be a connection between your anxiety and the amount of caffeine you consume? If so, I encourage you to determine how much caffeine is suitable for you.

Second, are you sensitive to the effects of caffeine? I am. If I consume caffeine after 1:00 p.m., my sleep is significantly affected. If I drink more than one cup of coffee, I will be shaky and uptight all day. My husband can drink an espresso after dinner and fall asleep two hours later. What about you? I will discuss caffeine concerning sleep in the next chapter.

Hydration
Every system in the body needs water to function, including the brain. About 75 percent of our brain tissue is water. We need to consume a sufficient amount of water to help our brains work well. Not drinking enough water causes our brain function to slow down. Dehydration also causes stress on our bodies, which can increase anxiety symptoms. Also, water contributes to the production of hormones and neurotransmitters, specifically serotonin (the happy chemical). It boosts our immune system, makes minerals and vitamins more accessible, improves mood, flushes out toxins, and increases energy levels. Most of us need to drink more water. We should consume at least ten cups a day and more when we exercise. I am constantly behind in my water intake. How about you?

Mild to moderate dehydration symptoms are thirst, dark yellow urine (note that vitamin B causes urine to be bright yellow), feeling dizzy, dry mouth, lips, and eyes, urinating less than four times a day, moodiness, difficulty concentrating, and headaches. I can't emphasize enough how crucial staying hydrated is.

Blood Sugar

Another issue related to nutrition and mental health is blood sugar regulation. Blood sugar problems can significantly affect mood. If you are like me, when your blood sugar drops, you become agitated. When I get irritable, the first thing my husband or close friends ask is, "When was the last time you ate?" You can probably imagine my response, since I am already irritated. We maintain healthy blood sugar by eating regularly (three meals and one or two healthy snacks). The problem I have is, when I get famished, I don't care what I eat as long as I am eating something. So plan accordingly whenever possible. Another way to keep blood sugar regulated is to eat protein at every meal and exercise regularly.

Inflammation

Lastly, we need to talk about inflammation. This topic is more related to depression, but there can be some correlation to anxiety. Inflammation is a hot topic these days and is often discussed in a negative light. However, inflammation is essential to our health—our body's natural response to a threat, such as an injury, virus, or bacteria. It is crucial to healing and immune function. If you get a nasty cut on your hand, the area will swell, which is part of the process to protect the injured area from infection and help heal the wound.

Inflammation also occurs when there is a threat of danger. As discussed earlier, our amygdala triggers the fight-flight-freeze response when there is a real or perceived threat, which then floods us with adrenaline. The adrenaline helps us escape or fight off danger.

However, when we regularly face this stress response, our bodies create too much inflammation, wreaking havoc on our bodies and brains. When inflammation is out of balance, specific pathways become overactive, creating fatigue, pain, emotional symptoms of irritability, depression, anxiety, and insomnia. A few of the physical problems caused by inflammation are heart disease, higher risk for cancer, Alzheimer's, joint issues, gut problems, lung problems, and sleep issues.

Besides too much stress, some of the known causes of inflammation are food sensitivities, allergies, dysbiosis (imbalance of bacteria in the gut), toxins, drug side-effects, drug addictions, and trauma. The trauma can be either physical or emotional. One of the best ways to balance inflammation is through diet. The diet is similar to what we have already discussed, but add the spice turmeric when possible. Turmeric has some anti-inflammatory benefits. In addition to the spice, you can purchase turmeric in pill form and use it as a supplement. Also, filtered water is beneficial. Use organic foods whenever possible and avoid processed foods. If you want more information on a diet to reduce inflammation, look up Dr. Andrew Weil, who has some great books on diet and inflammation. I like him because he allows occasional pasta and dark chocolate.

Application:

Write what areas of nutrition you might need to implement in your daily life. Then prioritize the list, and commit to adding one item each week.

Questions:

1. What information surprised you the most in this chapter? Why?

_____

_____

_____

2. What will be the most challenging idea for you to implement into your diet? Why? What would make it easier?

_____

_____

_____

CHAPTER 15
SLEEP

A ruffled mind makes a restless pillow.
— *Charlotte Bronte*

My oldest son struggled with sleep when he was a boy. When he was in kindergarten, I taught him muscle relaxation and deep breathing exercises. One night, I walked by his room and heard him taking slow, deep breaths to help himself fall asleep. Sometimes, when he was ready for bed, he asked me to go through the muscle-relaxation techniques with him. It helped him relax and doze off. I taped a notecard on his ceiling (he was on the top bunk) that read, *So do not fear, for I am with you; do not be dismayed, for I am your God. I will strengthen you and help you; I will uphold you with my righteous right hand* (Isaiah 41:10).

Most people do not get enough sleep, especially good sleep. Sleep deprivation has become a serious problem for Americans. One-third of U.S. adults sleep less than the recommended seven to eight hours daily, and 40 percent report feeling drowsy during the day.[63] Approximately seventy million Americans suffer from a sleep disorder.[64]Mathew Walker, Ph.D., a sleep specialist, says, "I used to suggest that sleep is the third pillar of good health, along with diet and exercise, but I don't agree with that anymore. Sleep is the single most effective thing you can do to reset your brain and body for health."[65]

We cannot survive without sleep. Here are some of the benefits of good sleep: mood regulation, stress relief, improved mood, increased energy, improved concentration and productivity, and physical healing. Good sleep also helps prevent weight gain, lowers the risk of heart disease, diabetes, and dementia, and it improves our immune system.

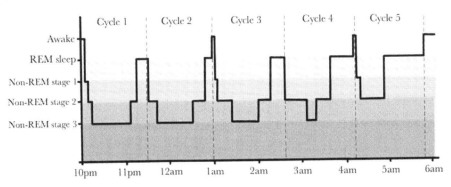

To better understand how sleep works, I will briefly explain our sleep cycle using the graph above. There are four stages of sleep. The first three stages are called Non-REM (Rapid Eye Movement) sleep, and the fourth is called REM sleep.

- Stage 1: This occurs as we are preparing to fall asleep. During this stage, we are easily awakened—Stage 1 lasts five to ten minutes.
- Stage 2: This is light sleep. Our heart rate begins to slow, and our body temperature drops slightly.
- Stage 3: This is where deep sleep occurs. It is harder to be awakened during this stage. If we were to wake up during deep sleep, we might feel disoriented. During stage 3, the body repairs and promotes bone and tissue growth, increases blood supply to the muscles, and strengthens the immune system.

- Stage 4: This is REM sleep. Usually, the first REM sleep cycle happens about ninety minutes after we fall asleep and lasts approximately ten minutes. It is crucial to understand that each REM cycle lasts longer than the one before. The last REM cycle can last up to an hour. Stage 4 is when most of our dreams occur. REM sleep is essential for emotional regulation and memory. During stage 4, our events of the day are stripped of some of the emotions, which allows us to recall an experience without actually reliving it. REM is crucial for our mental health.

Ideally, we go through four or five sleep cycles a night. If we awaken in the night for an extended period, our sleep cycle starts over, going back to cycle one. This means we will get less REM sleep, which is a crucial stage for our mental health.

Anyone who has experienced sleep deprivation knows how it can affect us physically, emotionally, and mentally. We may become cranky when we are tired. Lack of sleep and poor sleep quality can manifest as depression, anxiety, ADHD, and other mental health issues. Sleep deprivation increases activity in the amygdala. When we are not getting enough good sleep, our amygdala goes into overdrive. Also, lack of sleep can cause problems with the communication between the amygdala and the prefrontal cortex. Severe sleep deprivation can even cause psychosis (lost contact with reality).

"Sleep is vital for memory. During sleep, especially the cycles of deep dream sleep, the brain doesn't just revisit the events of the day in a more organized way. It also works on processing the emotions attached to these recollections. When a memory is filed away during sleep, it's also stripped of some of the powerful feelings—like fear, grief, anger, and joy—that might have clouded the experiences in the heat of the moment."[66] Sleep disturbances are a serious problem. Not only do sleep problems cause physical and mental issues, but depression, anxiety, and other psychological and physical health problems can cause sleep disturbance.

Caffeine and Sleep

Fortunately, there are things we can do to increase our likelihood of better sleep. The first is caffeine reduction. For many, this idea seems impossible, because caffeine is what helps you get through your busy days. However, this mentality can cause a vicious cycle of sleep deprivation and increased caffeine intake. If you do not struggle with sleep, you can skip this part, but if you do, keep reading. "Even one cup of coffee or caffeinated tea in the morning can affect sleep for forty-eight hours."[67] Yikes! As I have studied this issue, I have learned that caffeine can affect both falling asleep and causing us to awaken in the night. Caffeine can block the first cycle of deep sleep and additional cycles if there is a significant amount of caffeine in our system. Caffeine's physical reactions are similar to the biological response to fear. Both can leave us feeling jittery, short of breath, and agitated. So if you ingest caffeine and have sleep issues, take a courageous step and abstain for a week or two and see if it helps.

Dr. Anne Procyk gives the following expectations for eliminating caffeine:

- Days 1–3: Generally, people feel tired, sluggish, moody, foggy-headed, unfocused, and have a headache for part of it.
- Days 4–7: People start to feel better, with improved energy, clearer focus, less waking at night, and falling asleep more easily.

Within a week, most people feel great, and sleep has improved.[68]

Alcohol and Sleep

Did you know that alcohol is the number one sleep-aid in the United States? Twenty percent of American adults rely on alcohol to fall asleep. Alcohol may help a person fall asleep, but it can also wake you in the night and decrease REM sleep. Research shows that when alcohol leaves the body, it leaves the nervous system in an agitated state, which can awaken some people. Also, a moderate amount of alcohol an hour before bed can reduce melatonin production by nearly 20 percent, which affects sleep.[69] Alcohol affects the circadian rhythm that governs our twenty-four-hour sleep cycle. The more alcohol consumed and the closer you drink before bed, the more it will negatively affect sleep.

Sleep Aids
Nearly nine million U.S. adults take prescription sleep aids. The numbers are much higher for those using over-the-counter sleep aids. The number of adults using sleep aids increases with age. There are a couple of things to consider when using a sleep aid. Like alcohol, sleep aids can lower the amount of restorative sleep a person gets. Second, using a sleep aid regularly can prevent you from determining the underlying issues causing the sleep problem.

Nighttime Routine
If you have children, you know the benefits of having a nighttime routine to help them wind down. As adults, we too can benefit from having a bedtime routine. After a bedtime routine becomes a habit, our bodies will connect the routine with sleep, which will cause our bodies to prepare for sleep. A bedtime routine consists of activities you need to accomplish before bed, such as brushing your teeth, washing your face, showering, and exercises that relax you. Going to bed in a cool environment promotes sleep. Calming activities may include deep breathing, muscle relaxation, meditation, a warm bath, or reading (something calm and not on a device). Besides performing relaxing activities before bed, we want to avoid highly stimulating activities prior to sleep. This does not include sex, which can improve sleep. Most people find it difficult to go from doing something active and stimulating to falling asleep, including exercise, watching an intense show or movie, or reading a scary book.

For many years my house was full of men. We watched shoot-'em-up shows and shows about wild beasts that kill other wild animals or humans, for that matter. The boys looked forward to "Shark Week" all year. There was a time when I gave up on my rule of absolutely, positively no pay-per-view boxing or cage fighting. Please don't judge me. And take note, I never watch it and try not to even listen to it. Just hearing it can keep me up at night. Don't do what my family does every so often and watch crazy material right before bed. It affects your sleep.

Healthy Diet and Sleep

A healthy diet (see Chapter 14) can improve sleep. There are a few vitamin and mineral deficiencies linked to sleep problems. They are vitamins B3, B5, B6, B9, B12, D, and E, and the minerals niacin, magnesium, potassium, calcium, and iron. Always check with your doctor before adding supplements to your diet. It is possible to take too much iron and the fat-soluble vitamins A, D, E, and K.[70]

Daytime Exercise

Daytime exercise (see Chapter 13) is crucial for good sleep. I say *daytime* exercise, because many people have difficulty falling asleep if they exercise in the evening. If this doesn't happen to you, then by all means, exercise whenever it is most convenient. Charlene Gamalso, medical director of Johns Hopkins Center for Sleep, says, "We have solid evidence that exercise does, in fact, help you fall asleep more quickly and improves sleep quality."[71] The good news is, we can see the benefit of thirty minutes of moderate exercise on our sleep the same night. Both exercise and sleep calm the amygdala, which makes reducing anxiety much more manageable.

Some people's sleep difficulty is due to a deficiency of melatonin, a hormone we produce naturally that regulates sleep. Melatonin, also known as the sleep hormone, has a significant role in our circadian rhythm. Its production and release are connected to darkness. The darkness signals our brains to release melatonin, and light from TV, cell phones, and computer screens halt production.[72] Exposing yourself to daylight in the morning can help keep your sleep cycle on track.

Melatonin

If your sleep difficulty is due to melatonin deficiency, try taking a natural supplement of melatonin. Studies have found that a melatonin supplement can shorten the time it takes to fall asleep, lengthens sleep time, and enhances sleep quality.[73] Melatonin can be taken in doses between 0.5 to 10 mg per day. Start with a low amount and increase as needed. It's best taken a half an hour to an hour before bed. Melatonin also works well for jet lag and shift work.

Screen Time

Avoid screen time for an hour before bed. The light from screens, including your cell phone, can affect your body's circadian rhythm. That light makes your brain think it is still daylight, and therefore the brain doesn't release melatonin. As best you can before bed, avoid TV, computers, cell phones, game stations, Kindles, iPads, or other devices with this artificial light.

If none of these ideas work for you and sleep is still a problem, talk to your doctor and consider doing a sleep study to figure out what is causing your sleep issues. Good sleep is a key factor to reducing an over-active amygdala.

Application:

If you struggle with sleep, write which tips you will try first, second, and third. Then commit to trying number one in the next two days.

Questions:

1. What bad habits might you have that could affect your sleep?

_____

_____

_____

2. How many hours of sleep do you get a night? Do you feel rested when you wake up? If not, which of the above activities have you tried?

_____

_____

_____

Chapter 16
Making New Habits

We sow a thought and reap an act; we sow an act and reap a habit; we sow a habit and reap a character; we sow a character and reap a destiny. — Ralph Waldo Emerson

We have discussed many ways we can take every thought captive to reduce anxiety. As I mentioned in the Introduction, for change to occur, we must take action. We must follow through with what we have learned. Some of us have a hard time doing what we know is good for us. Most of us know that eating healthy is smart, and exercise will keep our bodies and minds stronger. Yet most Americans don't do these things regularly. So why don't most of us follow through with healthy habits? Could it be distorted thinking? Maybe you think you are not worth it, or you don't have the time. But you are worth it, and your physical and mental health requires attention. Maybe you lack discipline in your life. How would you answer the question? Whatever the reason, let's look at ways to add positive habits to our daily routine, lower our anxiety, and keep ourselves healthier mentally, physically, and spiritually.

First, it is essential not to add all of these exercises at once. That is not realistic and will leave you feeling discouraged. Take one or two ideas and start implementing them. I recommend picking a Bible verse that touched your heart and meditating on it daily for a week. Practice deep breathing throughout each day. If you don't already exercise regularly, go walking with a friend. Maybe add more vegetables to your dinner on a couple of nights. Continue to add other techniques that sound beneficial to you.

Start a gratitude journal the following week. After you have chosen a few relaxation techniques that you find beneficial, ponder what one or two of your core beliefs might be. Pay attention to your automatic thoughts that create anxiety. Go through some of the cognitive-behavioral practices and take notes. If possible, find a trusted friend to go through these techniques alongside you. Chances are, you know someone who struggles with anxiety too.

Eric Greitens wrote this about implementing habits: "When a habit has become so ingrained that actions begin to flow from you without conscious thought or effort, then you have changed your character. If we are intentional about what we repeatedly do, we can practice who we want to become. And through practice, we can become who we want to be." He also said, "Remember that deciding is not doing, and wanting is not choosing. Transformation will take place not because of what you decide you want, but because of what you choose to do."[74] The key to developing new habits is repetition, not perfection. What we do repeatedly becomes automatic. Developing positive thought habits is how we formulate automatic thoughts.

Remember, the more we respond to thoughts with anxiety, the deeper the anxiety becomes wired into our brain, which develops harmful habits of thinking. We can use this wiring technique for our benefit with positive patterns of thinking. We can make new neuropathways by intentionally and repetitively following the apostle Paul's advice: "Whatever is true, whatever is noble, whatever is right, whatever is pure, whatever is lovely, whatever is admirable—if anything is excellent or praiseworthy—think about such things" (Philippians 4:8).

Change happens through intentional practice and repetition. Let me say that again: "Change happens through *intentional* practice and repetition." Deliberate practice means to do something on purpose. Put it in your schedule; write it on your calendar. *Just Do It.*

I have a photo of my son Drew when he was maybe eighteen months old. He was climbing up the pantry, wearing a white T-shirt that said, *Just Do It.* His feet were on the third shelf, and his hands were reaching into the highest shelf, searching for something— probably cookies. It was a scary sight, because he was so tiny and yet so high off the floor. The photo reminds me to take action even if it's a little scary, even if it takes time, and even if I don't want to. Repetition means to do it over and over again. We do not master anything without repetition. Nothing worth anything comes easily. Remember, our cups are filled drop-by-drop, so begin the process one hour and one day at a time.

My original desire in writing this book was to make a Bible study, because going through these exercises in a group setting offers the opportunity for accountability. It would also make it easier to share our stories with others. I encourage you not to go this alone if at all possible. If you don't believe you have someone to communicate with and be accountable to, that's okay. Do the work. Write your story. Make a journal of all the activities you complete. Set goals, and pat yourself on the back when you accomplish them. You are a child of God, and you are worth it.

Here are a few tips on building new habits:

- Choose one or two habits at a time.
- Know why you are making the changes you want to make. You are worth it. You have decided you want to take your thoughts captive to reduce your anxiety.
- Use reminders. Make a time each day when you will practice a technique or work on an exercise. Set the alarm on your phone. I have an app on my phone that reminds me to take deep breaths.

- Reward yourself. Maybe not with chocolate cake but with a walk on the beach or something else you enjoy.
- Be accountable as much as possible.
- When you stumble, give yourself grace and know tomorrow is a new day.
- Be patient. Over time, as we make these daily choices, we will find ourselves less anxious. Becoming healthier physically, emotionally, and spiritually is a life-long process.

As you practice the various exercises discussed in this book, give yourself grace in developing new habits. It takes time to create new patterns. I love the analogy James Clear uses in his book, *Atomic Habits: An Easy & Proven Way to Build Good Habits & Break Bad Ones.* He asks the reader to imagine looking at an ice cube on a table in a twenty-five-degree room. Very slowly, the room begins to warm to 26 degrees. Then 27 . . . 28 . . . The ice cube hasn't moved. It is still as solid as a rock. Soon it is 29 degrees. Then 30 . . . 31 . . . yet nothing. Suddenly the room is at 32 degrees. The ice begins to melt. A 1-degree shift changes everything.[75] Even when you don't see a lot of change, keep going. Change will happen. Remember, many of you have been experiencing anxiety for a long time. It has become habitual. Keep working on healing. Do not give up. You are worth it!

Renewed minds and positive habits are a necessity to lives pressing onward in victory.[76] We can have victory over anxiety.

The Journey of a thousand miles begins with one step. — Lao Tzu

Application:

Write two or three exercises from *Victory Over Anxiety* that you want to make habits.

Questions:

1. What is the most challenging aspect of creating a new habit? What roadblocks might keep you from following through with the healthy habits you want to make in your daily life?

_____

_____

_____

2. What harmful habit(s) do you need to extinguish? What obstacles might come up that will make eradicating any of these habits more challenging?

_____

_____

_____

Chapter 17
What Does God Say about Anxiety?

Do not be afraid!
— Jesus

As soon as the meal was finished, Jesus insisted that the disciples get into the boat and go to the other side of the lake while he dismissed the people. After the crowd had dispersed, he climbed the mountain so he could be by himself and pray. He remained there alone, late into the night.

The disciples in their boat were far out to sea when a strong headwind arose, and they were held back by the waves.

At about four o'clock in the morning, Jesus came toward them, walking on the water. They were scared to death.

"A ghost!" they said, crying out in terror.

Jesus was quick to comfort them. "Take courage. It is I. Do not be afraid."

Peter boldly said, "Master, if it's really you, call me to come to you on the water."

"Come," Jesus said.

Peter jumped out of the boat and walked on the water toward Jesus. As he saw the waves churning beneath his feet, he became afraid and began to sink. "Master! Save me!"

Immediately, Jesus reached down and grabbed his hand. "Oh, you of weak faith. Why did you doubt?"

The two of them climbed into the boat, and the wind calmed.

The disciples in the boat had seen everything that had happened. Totally amazed and worshipful, they said, "Without a doubt, you are the Son of God"(Matthew 14:22–33 author paraphrase).

The Bible mentions anxiety or fear more than 300 times. The most repeated command Jesus makes is, "Do not be afraid." He says it seventy times in the *New International Version*. Why do you think Jesus mentions fear so much? Could it be that he knows how much we struggle with anxiety?

Here are a handful of the meditation verses that mention anxiety and fear:

- Anxiety weighs down the heart, but a kind word cheers it up. — Proverbs 12:25
  This verse gives us a fact about anxiety. It weighs us down. We all need to remember how true this is.
- Peace I leave with you; my peace I give you. I do not give to you as the world gives. Do not let your hearts be troubled and do not be afraid. — John 14:27
  Here we hear directly from Jesus. As you will see in Philippians 4:6, God talks about anxiety and peace in the same verse. He compassionately wants us to have peace, not anxiety. He is not condemning us but rather desires good things for us.
- Jesus came and touched them. "Get up," he said. "Don't be afraid." — Matthew 17:7
  Here Jesus is responding to the disciples falling to the ground because they were terrified after hearing God the Father's audible voice. Jesus lovingly touches them and says, "Don't be afraid." Of course, they were already afraid, and they would be again, but Jesus reassures them that they don't *need* to fear because he is with them.

- Do not fear, for I am with you; do not be dismayed, for I am your God. I will strengthen you and help you; I will uphold you with my righteous right hand. — Isaiah 41:10
  This verse was my son's favorite, giving him peace in knowing God's promises. He is with us; he is our God, he will strengthen us, he will help us, he will hold us. Oh, the faith of a child.
- Do not be anxious about anything, but in every situation, by prayer and petition, with thanksgiving, present your requests to God. — Philippians 4:6

Philippians 4:6 and the verses that follow are worth further discussion. God tells us, "Don't be anxious," but he also tells us what to do when we are afraid.

Read the following passage and meditate on what God is saying to you.

"Do not be anxious about anything, but in everything by prayer and petition with thanksgiving present your requests to God. And the peace of God, which transcends all understanding, will guard your hearts and your minds in Christ Jesus. Finally, brothers, whatever is true, whatever is noble, whatever is right, whatever is pure, whatever is lovely, whatever is admirable, if anything is excellent or praiseworthy, think about such things. Whatever you have learned or received or heard from me, or seen, put it into practice. And the God of peace will be with you" (Philippians. 4:6–9).

Verse six tells us not to be anxious about anything. In light of who God is and who we are as his children, there is nothing we need to be anxious about. In everything by "prayer and petition with thanksgiving" we can present our requests to God. He wants us to go before him with our concerns, no matter what they are. By doing this, we will have the peace of God that goes beyond what our anxiety is telling us. This peace will guard our hearts and minds.

Oh, how we need Jesus to guard our hearts and minds. God's peace is more than the human mind can fully understand. We may not understand it, but we can experience it if we will let God boost our confidence that he watches over us. If we know we will spend eternity with him, we don't even have to fear death.

We need to focus our thoughts on godly, noble, and praiseworthy things. As we do that, verse nine says "the God of peace will be with us." God is always with us. We can learn to do this. We can take our anxious thoughts captive and think about godly things.

We are told to renew our minds. "I urge you, brothers and sisters, in view of God's mercy, to offer your bodies as a living sacrifice, holy and pleasing to God. This is your true and proper worship. Do not conform to the pattern of this world, but be transformed by *the renewing of your mind.* Then you will be able to test and approve what God's will is; his good, pleasing and perfect will" (Romans 12:1–2 *emphasis added*).

We can properly worship our Father by sacrificing our bodies. We do this by not conforming to this world but allowing God to transform us by the renewing of our minds. Then we will know what God's perfect will is for us. Isn't that incredibly exciting?

Jesus understands and has compassion when we experience anxiety.

One day, Jesus and his disciples were again out on the sea. Suddenly, a furious storm came, and the waves were about to capsize the boat. But Jesus was sleeping. The disciples awakened him, saying, "'Lord, help! We're about to drown!" They were afraid, because the situation really was serious. But Jesus wasn't afraid. "You of little faith," he said. "Why are you so afraid?" He rebuked the winds and the waves, and it was completely calm. The disciples were amazed. "What kind of man is this?" they said. "Even the wind and waves obey him (Matthew 8:23–27 author paraphrase).

The disciples were scared to death. While walking with Jesus, they still experienced fear and anxiety. So it's understandable that even though Jesus is always with us, we too will experience anxiety.

One of the interesting parts of this story is the Greek word *seismos,* which Matthew uses to describe the storm. Matthew uses this word only two other times in Scripture, once when Jesus died and again at his resurrection: "At the moment the curtain of the temple was torn in two from top to bottom. The earth shook (*seismos*), and the rocks split" (Matthew 27:51). "There was a violent earthquake (*seismos*), for an angel of the Lord came down from heaven and, going to the tomb, rolled back the stone and sat on it" (Mathew 28:2). So Matthew describes the power of the storm in chapter eight using the same term he used to describe the shaking earth at the death and the resurrection of Jesus. That is a powerful storm.

Did you notice something unusual about this story? Jesus was sleeping during a mighty storm. Do you ever feel like Jesus is sleeping while you are going through a challenging situation? I do. In full panic mode, the disciples awakened Jesus screaming that they were about to drown. When that story is described in Mark 4:38, the disciples are questioning his love for them. I've done that too. How does Jesus answer their concern? "You of little faith. Why are you so afraid?" This storm was violent, yet Jesus says, "Why are you afraid?" He can ask this because he knows the storm is no big deal. In every storm in our lives, we don't have to be afraid if we know Jesus is in control. We will be okay. Even if we were to die, we would be in Heaven and would never want to come back to Earth. When we fear as the disciples did, we lack faith in God's ability to respond to our storm. We often forget he has great plans for our lives.

Great men and women of the Bible experienced fear. It started with Adam and Eve. They walked and talked with the Father, but they experienced fear and shame after sin. (Genesis 3:10).

Abraham experienced anxiety many times, and God considered him a man of great faith (Hebrew 11:8). Abraham fled to Egypt for fear of a famine (Genesis 12:10), and then he feared the Egyptians because his wife Sarai (Sarah) was beautiful. He thought they would kill him and take her for themselves (Genesis 12:11–20). Abraham showed the same anxiety in Genesis 20, when he told King Abimelech that Sarah was his sister.

Elijah, an amazing prophet of God, was afraid of Jezebel (1 Kings 19).

Queen Esther was afraid to approach her husband, the king, to save her people from destruction (Esther 4).

King David, a man after God's own heart, was often afraid. In Psalm 55:5, he says, "Fear and trembling have beset me; horror has overwhelmed me." After seeing the power of God in his life many times, he still trembled in fear.

Mary, the mother of Jesus, was afraid when the angel came to tell her God's plan (Luke 1:29).

All the disciples abandoned Jesus out of fear. Out of fear, Peter denied Jesus three times (John 18:17, 25, 27).

There is *no* condemnation here. There is *no* judgment. I have been a believer for over thirty-five years, and a psychologist for over twenty-five years, and I struggle with anxiety. Too often, I still think on things that are *not* pure, *not* noble, *not* lovely, and *not* praiseworthy. Just because we read the Word of God does not mean we automatically do everything it says. I wish it were that easy. Even the apostle Paul said, "What I want to do, I do not do, but what I hate I do" (Romans 7:15).

God's Word does heal. When we are willing, God uses his Spirit to work in our hearts and minds through his Word to make changes within us. There is hope for us in Christ Jesus.

My prayer for you is the same prayer that the apostle Paul had for the Thessalonians: "Now may the Lord of peace himself give you peace at all times and in every way. The Lord be with all of you" (2 Thessalonians 3:16).

Application:

For a couple of minutes, meditate on one of the scripture verses we discussed in this chapter. Ask yourself three questions: *What is God saying in the verse? What is God saying about himself in the verse? And what may God be saying to me?*

Questions:
1. Did any of the verses in this chapter catch your attention? What were your thoughts when you read them? Did you experience any feelings of shame or condemnation as you read? Write your thoughts and feelings and share them with God. He wants to hear from you and can handle anything you bring to him.

_____

_____

_____

2. Were you encouraged by all the godly men and women in the Bible, who experienced fear and anxiety? What thoughts did you have when you read about them?

_____

_____

_____

HEARTFELT THANKS

What an amazing group of people I have in my life. First, I want to thank my husband, Patrick. You have been an incredible support to me throughout our marriage. If it were not for your support during my doctorate program, I never would have finished. You supported me as a stay-at-home mom, and now you are my number one advocate as I write, teach, and do what I love.

Second, I want to thank my boys. J.P. and Drew, I love being your mom. It has been so fun raising you. What wonderful young men you have become. Thanks for all your support over the years and for providing me with so many great stories.

To my parents, John and Sandie Drew: I am heartbroken that Dad didn't get a chance to see *Victory Over Anxiety* published, but I know he is very proud. Mom, you have been my inspiration. You have shown me how to be loved and to love. I am the woman I am today because of your love and encouragement.

To my siblings, Tina, David, and Darren: What fun we had growing up, even amid the challenges we faced. I am beyond blessed to have three siblings that I love spending time with. Tina, I didn't get to pick you as my sister, but I did choose you as my dearest friend. I love our regular hikes and all the memories we have made cycling thousands of miles over the years.

I always say that being in community is the most important thing we can do for our mental health. To my TAG (Tuesday Accountability Group) besties: Brooke, Susie, and Betty, I'm so thankful to do life with you. When God says, "Iron sharpens iron, so a friend sharpens a friend" (Proverbs 27:17), he had you in mind. The three of you have sharpened me and helped me become a woman of God. Thank you for loving me in my darkest times and celebrating with me in my most joyful moments.

To my writer's group, Nancy A., Tonya, Nancy K., Julie, and Cindy: Thanks for encouraging me in my writing. When I wanted to stop, you kept me going. Nancy A., thanks for your support in my teaching endeavors. You have been such a support to me. Tonya, thank you for all your wisdom and kindness. You are always available to help and encourage me. Nancy K., you have been an excellent example to me. Your love for God is evident in everything you do. Julie, you give the best hugs of anyone I know, and your creativity inspires me. Cindy, your diligence in writing has motivated me.

To my editor Frank Ball: I know this project was a lot of work. My gifts are encouraging others, teaching people how to reduce anxiety, and a few other things, but punctuation is not one of them. Thank you for the hours you spent fixing my errors and helping me get my point across.

Thank you to a few friends who have come alongside me over the years and have done life with me. Kamii, we have been good friends since the fourth grade. We have so many beautiful memories together. Whenever I think of you, I smile. Jodi, you helped change the trajectory of my life by helping me develop the athlete in me. You are a trusted friend. Camden, you taught me how to share my heart with another human. Thank you for that gift and all the laughs we shared over the years.

Thank you, Brooke. You have been such a dear friend. We are two peas in a pod, and I am grateful for our friendship.

To my Bible study ladies, what fun we have had studying God's Word together and praying for one another. Thanks to my church family at Calvary Church, Santa Ana. You have been a great support to my family and me.

Lastly, but most importantly, thank you, Jesus, for your love and grace. You are my rock.

ABOUT THE AUTHOR

Dr. Andrea Ganahl is a licensed clinical psychologist specializing in anxiety. She teaches classes on how to reduce anxiety at churches, women's groups, and college campuses. Andrea has written articles for Focus on the Family magazines.

Andrea and her husband, Patrick, live in Southern California with their chocolate Labrador, Mollie. They have two adult sons.

You can find her at **Instagram.com/VictoryOverAnxiety**, **Facebook.com/Dr.AndreaGanahl**, or her website at **AndreaGanahl.com**.

ENDNOTES

Section I Introduction

[1] John Kavanaugh, *The Word Engaged: Meditation on the Sunday Scriptures* (Maryknoll,NY, Orbis Books, 1997) 110.

Chapter 1 What Is Anxiety? and What Are the Causes?

[2] htpps://www.Learnersdictionary.com/definition/anxiety

[3] Ibid

[4] https://www.elementsbehavioralhealth.com/mental-health/8-facts-anxiety-anxiety-disorders/

[5] https://adaa.org/about-adaa/press-room/facts-statistics.

[6] *Desk Reference to the Diagnostic Criteria from DSM-5* (Arlington, VA, American Psychiatric Association, 2013)

[7] https://adaa.org/about-adaa/press-room/facts-statistics.

[8] Ibid

[9] https://www.elementsbehavioralhealth.com/mental-health/8-facts-anxiety-anxiety-disorders/

[10] *Desk Reference to the Diagnostic Criteria from DSM-5* (Arlington, VA, American Psychiatric Association, 2013)

[11] https://adaa.org/about-adaa/press-room/facts-statistics.

[12] Ibid

[13] https://www.elementsbehavioralhealth.com/mental-health/8-facts-anxiety-anxiety-disorders/

[14] *Desk Reference to the Diagnostic Criteria from DSM-5* (Arlington, VA, American Psychiatric Association, 2013)

[15] https://adaa.org/about-adaa/press-room/facts-statistics.

[16] *Desk Reference to the Diagnostic Criteria from DSM-5* (Arlington, VA, American Psychiatric Association, 2013)

[17] https://adaa.org/about-adaa/press-room/facts-statistics.

[18] https://www.medicalnewstoday.com/articles/trauma#definition

[19] https://www.medicalnewstoday.com/articles/trauma#childhood-trauma

[20] https://www.nami.org/blogs/NAMI-blog/january-2018/The-comorbidity-of-anxiety-and-depression

[21] https://www.summitmedicalgroup.com/library/adult_health/bha_substance_induced_anxiety_disorders/

Chapter 2 Essential Brain Fujnctions Regarding Anxiety
[22] Gavin De Becker, The Gift of Fear: And Other Survival Signals That Protect Us From Violence (New York, NY, Dell Publishing, 1997) 301.

Chapter 3 There Is Hope: The Wiring and Rewiring of Our Brains
[23] https://en.wikipedia.org/wiki/Hebbian_theory

Section II How to Take Your Anxious Thoughts Captive

Chapter 4 Three Steps to Change How We Think
[24] Rick Warren, *The Daniel Plan* (Grand Rapids, MI, Zondervan, 2013)

Chapter 5 Why Do We Think the Way We Do?
[25] Eric Greitens, *Resilience: Hard-Won Wisdom for Living a Better Life* (New York, NY, First Mariner Books, 2015)

Chapter 6 Determining Our Core Beliefs
[26] David Burns, M.D., *The Feeling Good Handbook* (New York, NY, Penguin Group, 1999)

Chapter 7 Memory
[27] Dr. Curt Thompson, *Anatomy of the Soul* (Carrollton, TX, Tyndale, 2010)
[28] Daniel J. Soegel, M.D., *Brainstorm: Power and Purpose of the TeenageBrain* (New York, NY, Penguin Group, 2013) 113-114
[29] Victor E. Frankl, Man's Search for Meaning (Boston, MA, Beason Press, 2006)
[30] Dr. Curt Thompson, *Anatomy of the Soul* (Carrollton, TX, Tyndale, 2010)
[31] Ibid
[32] Ibid
[33] Mike Dubi, Patrick Powell, J. Eric Gentry, *Truama, PTSD, Greif & Loss: The Ten Core Competencies for Evidence-Based Treatment,* (Eau Claire, WI, PESI Publishing, 2017)
[34] Ibid

Chapter 8 Other Cognitive-Behavioral Techniques
[35] Eric Greitens, *Resilience: Hard-Won Wisdom for Living a Better Life* (New York, NY, First Mariner Books, 2015)
[36] Ibid
[37] https://www.health.harvard.edu/mind-and-mood/in-praise-of-gratitude
[38] Priscila Shirer, *Armor of God*, (Nashville, TN, Lifeway, 2015)

Chapter 9 Ways to Rewire Our Brains
[39] Henri Nouwen, Lifesigns: Intimacy, Fecundity, and Ecstasy In Christian Perspective, (New York, NY, Doubleday, 1986)
[40] Ann Voskamp, The Broken Way: A Daring Path into the Abundant Life (Grand Rapids, MN, Zondervan, 2016)
[41] Drs. Henry Cloud and John Townsend, *Safe People* (Grand Rapids, MI, Zondervan, 1995)

Section III Relaxation Techniques: The Beginning of Lowering Anxiety

Chapter 10 Meditation

[42] https://www.learnersdictionary.com/definition/meditation

[43] Richard Foster, *Celebration of Discipline*, (San Fransisco, CA, Harper & Row, 1988)

Chapter 11 Mindfulness

[44] Brennan Manning, *The Ragamuffin Gospel*, (Colorado Springs CO, Multnomah Publishers, 2005)

[45] https://www.mindful.org/10-mindful-attitudes-decrease-anxiety

[46] https://jamanetwork.com/journals/jamainternalmedicine/fullarticle/1809754

[47] Ibid

[48] https://www.sciencedirect.com/science/article/pii/016383439500025M

[49] https://blogs.scientificamerican.com/guest-blog/what-does-mindfulness-meditation-do-to-your-brain/

[50] https://hbr.org/2012/06/habits-why-we-do-what-we-do

Chapter 12 Other Relaxation Exercises

[51] https://www.health.harvard.edu/mind-and-mood/relaxation-techniques-breath-control-helps-quell-errant-stress-response

[52] Xochitl Dixon, Waiting for God: Trusting Daily in God's Plan and Pace, (Grand Rapis, MI, Discovery House, 2019).

[53] https://www.epainassist.com/fitness-and-exercise/progressive-muscle-relaxation

[54] https://www.healthline.com/health/affects-of-joy

[55] Rewritten from anonymous source, author unknown.

Section IV Life Style Modifications to Reduce Anxiety

Chapter 13 Physical Exercise

[56] http://www.heart.org/HEARTORG/HealthyLiving/PhysicalActivity/FitnessBasics/American-Heart-Association-Recommendations-for-Physical-Activity-in-Adults_UCM_307976_Article.jsp#.W0QnXtJKiUk

Chapter 14 Nutrition and Mental Health

[57] https://www.ncbi.nlm.nih.gov/pmc/articles/PMC4918317

[58] Anne Procyk, M.D., seminar handout: "Nutritional Treatments to Improve Mental Health Disorders: Non-Pharmaceutical Interventions for Depression, Anxiety, Bipolar & ADHD," (Eau Claire, WI, PESI Publishing, 2018)

[59] Ibid

[60] Ibid

[61] https://adaa.org/understanding-anxiety/socail-anxiety-disorder/socail-anxiety-and-alcohol-abuse

[62] http://www.Healthline.com/health/alcohol-and-anxiety

Chapter 15 Sleep

[63] http://time.com/4672988/the-sleep-cure-fountain-of-youth/

[64] https://americansleepfoundation.org/

[65] Ibid

[66] https://time.com.4672988/the-sleep-cure-fountain-of-youth/.

[67] Anne Procyk, M.D., Nutritional Treatments to Improve Mental Health Disorders: Non-Pharmaceutical Interventions for Depression, Anxiety, Bipolar & ADHD, (Eau Claire, WI, PESI Publsihing, 2018)

[68] ibid

[69] https://www.psychologytoday.com/us/blog/sleep-newzzz/201801/alcohol-and-sleep-what-you-need-know

[70] https://www.lifehack.org/832133/vitamins-for-sleep

[71] https://www.hopkinsmedicine.org/health/wellness-and-prevention/exercising-for-better-sleep

[72] https://www.netdoctor.co.uk/healthy-living/wellbeing/a34768876/melatonin/

[73] https://www.healthline.com/nutrition/melatonin#sleep

Chapter 16 Making New Habits

[74] Eric Greitens, *Resilience: Hard-Won Wisdom for Living a Better Life* (New York, NY, First Mariner Books, 2015)

[75] James Clear, Atomic Habits: An Easy & Proven Way to Build Good Habits & Break Bad Ones, (New York, NY, Avery, 2018).

[76] Beth Moore, Breaking Free: Discover the Victory of Total Surrender, (Nashville, TN, B&H Publishing, 2007)

Made in the USA
Columbia, SC
23 February 2025

54310351R00098